There are many things in all of our lives that can seem to be too powerful for us to tackle all by ourselves.

Sometimes we need to slow it all down and check, what exactly is going on?

There are some details I am certain of and have grown to learn throughout my own suffering or call it struggling if you will. The certainty is that not one of my feelings nor one of my thoughts will consume me beyond the point of existence.

I share with you some simple thoughts and scenarios to take a look at and perhaps you too can come to similar realizations.

LIFE is absolutely worth living.

Your life matters, you are important & you will make it through.

Chapters.

Introduction.

If you are like me and have many episodes in your life where you found yourself questioning LIFE, what it has in store for you and where is it all really going, then you probably have always wondered "how come there is no handbook for this?" I have never received any handbook either and thought why not share some of the simpler aspects of my day or life with you to help ease some of the questions in a way that can bring about a little inner peace and put an end to an overloaded mind of question after question. Hey if you are not like me in any way at all and have no racing mind ever then perhaps a little look at why it is going on for some of the rest of us might just help you and me become better friends.

Just as the title has suggested, "A layman's guide to Life" handbook is not the almighty almanac of the year or in any way a set of rules to live by, just a simple sneak peek into ourselves from a layman's point of view that could bring us to a better place in our daily living.

What does my life involve that could give me any position to write to you about how a life could be lived? I hear you ask; I have lived a unique life yet not in any way different to yours and so, a little about me.

As a teenager I lived a darker life of drug and alcohol abuse which led me to incarceration by the age of seventeen, which to be quite honest did not appear to me at the time to be anything out of the ordinary and just part of what we do as that was the life I was leading at the time. But now at 43 years of age I can clearly see it was definitely a wrong path that I was on and the lifestyle of such substance abuse, is today a horrifying thought. Being in prison and a judicial system was a very difficult time as a young man coming of age though it has shown me a greater understanding of myself at a very young age, this came by way of therapy and an adolescent treatment program.

By my early twenties I was a reformed man and became a young father (out of wedlock) though partnered with a wonderful girl. Young living and sober living as a young man. The beauty of being a father brought a certain peace to life that gave balance to the mixed-up world I had grown out of. The joys of fatherhood were wonderful and even though myself and my partner could not maintain our relationship we still had our beautiful son. Then dealing with the breakup and the emotional battle that it had led me to only enhanced the growth of life experiences on my path and it is with this look back on the how and why and when of the time that helps identify some reasoning to it all. As a young sober man, I went out and began to travel for work and travelled to faraway places being able to enjoy and experience new sights, new people and their thoughts and new ways of life. It seemed that life really had turned a corner and brought some of the most amazing people and highs into my own life.

I went on to be married to yet another wonderful girl and how lucky I was to have met not only one but a second wonderful person who was worth it so much that it felt only right to be married. My wife again opened my eyes up to new cultures and new experiences that I learned more about what love and life might actually mean. Like any young couple or new couple, we gave it our best shot and continued along a life of travel and adventure. This time not just me but my partner too. Marriage is not easy for everyone and there are times in everybody's relationships that just hit hard patches where the "gel with your partner" can fade away or just not happen. This happened for us and I found myself single again and out in the world. As you might remember I had been a person for asking questions of life and so I was back at it again, alone or single whichever you want to call it and out there travelling again. It is from a varied viewpoint that I have brought about this book to let you in on some of what I have learned to help you maybe just begin a little thought for yourself about your own life and see if there any things that I may have experienced that ring a bell for you that might just help you into a new place in your own happiness.

This is the hope that instead of continuing in a miserable existence or an unhappy one that you can hear me say some words that register/fit perfect for your own life. After all we have just one go around this merry go round and we might as well have a good go at it.

By my mid-thirties my beautiful son passed away from an unknown cause and just did not wake up for his school one Monday morning. He was only fifteen at the time, well three weeks after his fifteenth birthday actually and it was a definite difficult time. I know I have just now landed a block down on top of you and that thought you just had or perhaps the quick shiver of, what? The child died. Yes, I know, it has happened and yes you did read correctly but again the questions and the questions of life and to the universe. Where? Why? And all about what for?

These are very real and do not give me any credentials to speak to you about some of the questions that you have in your own life but are the reasons to share with you some of the thoughts we can have about the whole big theatre act of life and where a mind can go with its questioning

Within a few short years and lucky me with a third wonderful girl, a new relationship and a wonderful little baby boy. How awesome to become a father again and what worries come with that having been a grieving father already. There have been so many times that from out of one real tough emotional and mind wrecking time has come a beautiful new beginning that I wanted to share not just the events or happenings but the thoughts and the feelings that can be triggered in all of us, for some maybe even simpler reasons and you did not have to go through any devastating loss like I have to find yourself emotionally drained or mentally overloaded. Life can just get in the way sometimes and a busy day for one person might be a piece of cake for anyone else, a busy day for another may be the toughest thing we could ever do.

Within a couple of years, I lost my second son to a drowning accident, yes you heard me correctly, my second son has died too. When they say lightning cannot strike twice, well it has, and it is a major part or the reason I share with you my "layman's" thoughts and ideas of what life can be for any one of us at any time. Not only because of life experiences of loss and shock and horror. No, because of the daily battle that can be life when it appears there is no answer to anything. No answer to the questions of grief nor any answer to what it all means or how one simple life (mine) is meant to be.

I get it that we all have questions and we all have hardships and for these reasons I decided to write it out for you to bring a light of a different kind. A light on the subjects of how and why or try to uncover an understanding of what it is when our mind races. What exactly is going on when we find ourselves faced with changes or maybe you like to call them challenges. What is it when we cannot do simple things in daily life because we are emotionally screwed up or even dead? These are questions that can occur for anyone and there are no right or wrong answers, let us take a look at some of them and see if we together can reach an understanding of them.

It is not just loss or is it? When I look back, I can see loss of my own life as a teenager, to be taken away and locked up or the mini grief as a young father breaking up with his "baby momma" and having to be apart from his mighty first born. The loss involved in losing his wife and what a breakup of husband and wife actually does to a person.

Perhaps again to lose himself to new lands and the travel or the devastating loss of his first son. Yes, indeed this is the true loss and emotion of grief. To continue forward and find ways to piece it all together and rebuild on each occasion, find new life and grow out of each experience. Is it real growth if we are learning nothing? These are definitely reasons that I can now call myself an expert in the area of life and have to offer you a way in which to view things a little differently.

A second son to yet another graveyard and more grief, not just complicated life but the twist on the vision of what is real and what is not real can become so distorted that someone like me can truly say, anything is possible, nothing is impossible. Can a father be distant from his children and still love them with all his heart? Can any parent be involved in life while struggling in grief and continue to live? Can any one-person face life and its challenges to overcome them? Can any one person know what to do and when it is right to do it? Let's just say who really knows but we are going to explore some of the things that are worth exploring in the chapters that follow and it is with great pleasure I am going to dive into myself to share with you what can be and how I have found the reason to live, a reason beyond what you may have ever imagined and beyond normality without any excuses necessary. Come for the journey with me and let's see what might trigger for you as we take a look. It is with a smile on my face I welcome you to take this journey with me as I have brought about this written word to help you and me both see how wonderful life really is. Some tips on learning how to live despite all adversity that comes our way and some possible exercises of our minds to help calm us and bring about an inner peace.

It is not all sandal wearing and green tea drinking habits that can lead us to an inner peace and I assure you I do not own any tie dye t shirts. Just me, just like you, a person, a child of the world that has found some easier ways of doing the self-care and figuring out what so many things might actually be about.

Let us begin and if you can find a nice quiet place to get a little reading done, then I think we are on the right path already.

Thoughts & Emotions flow.

What is a thought in our head and its purpose to our life? Some of us think too much and others not enough. Yes I know you know and can pick out immediately in your head the people you know who fall into the category of "think not enough" but really though, what is this process inside of our brain that allow us a thought or where does it come from? What can trigger a thought? What can a thought do for us or more importantly what can we do with a thought?

When we think about anything too much it can consume us into maybe even a state of mind that can become like a frenzied mess of ourselves and bring us to the sanitarium. We could become a person who scribbles mathematical equations on a wall with chalk all day long in the corner of a hospital where it is policy to keep you under lock and key, all this from letting our thoughts run wild with us. Letting a thought run wild with us right inside of our head could trip the switch and we might never find our way back, that there is a crazy thought all in itself. So why do we not run wild in our mind every day or with every thought? I don't know is the truest answer I could give you.

Maybe we all have some sort of lettered illness or disease and just to be clear, there is no harm in having some letters or a condition that says we function differently, at least those who have been diagnosed have a half of an answer to their problems. What letters am I talking about? The OCD or ADHD kind of things, maybe we all have them in some shape or form, or letters of a different kind but a condition none the less. Maybe we all have some form or other of these classifications and could use pills to help. Help, now that is a word we can look at. What can we do for ourselves that might HELP us to see things clearer? I will have to introduce a scenario or two to try and decipher how we could use some techniques to manage a thought here or there.

The fact we have so many thoughts a second and so much goes on in our mind is "mind blowing" in itself. The beautiful thing to know is that all of our thoughts usually start off a little normal and makes us simply human. Yes, even those that do not think enough are human too.

What triggers a thought in us and what do we do with it and better yet, is there a process that means we "can't think straight"? Do we have to see a doctor because our head will not stay quiet long enough for us to catch our breath and are we in need of a little vacation trip to an asylum to just find "normal" again?

Again, it is a who knows kind of situation and best left between you and your doctor. What we can do though is find some ways to slow our thoughts down a little and not act on any wild thoughts impulsively. We can actually listen to our thoughts and give them their rightful place in our daily life.

Whether we are young or old does not make a difference to having thoughts and it has absolutely no influence what our race is either. We are human. Could we repeat that just for a second, WE ARE HUMAN. Thanks for repeating that. We have thoughts every day and we are human, that is about as simple as we can make it. So, it does make total sense that, we can have thoughts every day and this makes us human (agreed?), this is some good news already. We are not some form of alien just because we do not focus on our thoughts or because we do not know how to control them and we are not an alien just because we shift from one thought to another like a F1 race car driver shifts through gears. Nope, we are just plain old normal for having thoughts. Isn't this a relief to know we can consider ourselves "normal"?

Let's take an example or two like I had said, it will take some scenarios to try and shed a glimpse of light on the subject of thoughts just to try and gain a little understanding. I am a man and can only speak to you from my own understanding and point of view, this meaning women may have a different approach in how they form their own viewpoints or opinions on some things, but we are again like I said, HUMAN.

Let's just say I went into the city one day to the shopping district of the city and had in my mind the decision made to do some shopping. My plans are to buy myself some new clothes and do a little "treat myself" kind of day. I plan on heading for a particular place for lunch and have a plan of which bus to catch or what garage I will use to park in and have a nice plan for myself and my day. This would be a casual day and nothing but relaxing and a little me time to wander the streets and window shop more than my pocket will allow me, but I will spend what I can on myself and some new clothes and a nice lunch. These are my plans and I am feeling good about them.

I arrive into the city and the traffic is a little hectic, as always taxis are taking over the roads and I am having difficulty getting around the lanes. I finally cut a guy off and merge over to get into the parking garage and I have a few mutterings to myself because of how I see the other drivers being "the worst drivers" in the world. My car gets parked and off to high street shops I go, the poor driving of others and the traffic was not enough to shake me from my plans for the day and my thoughts are clear and my mind is focused on spoiling myself just a little. As I walk down the stairway to the high street I think for a moment, "what was the level I parked on?" No big deal I will just run back up and check just to be certain, I do not want to screw up my day after all. I didn't check the level when heading for the stairwell probably because of the little heat under my collar that I had for the poxy other drivers in the streets. So, it is level C and it is green coded. I might as well take the elevator back down as that is an easier way down and today is all about being nice to myself and so, off I go for my day out shopping. It is probably weird if you are a woman right now hearing me, a man, say something like "off out shopping" like a girl who has just gotten her first paycheck from her new job at the bank, but hey we guys shop too.

Let's take a minute though just to think ha-ha no, that think was not on purpose, let's think about what happened to our thinking a minute ago though. I was getting mad with other drivers in the traffic and I forgot to look and see what level I was parked on. Seems simple doesn't it? I did not take notice because my adrenaline was up a little bit and I got confused by what I needed to know, so I went back up which in turn has delayed me just a little. It is no big deal or no major delay but I wanted to pause on it for a minute to just see how something so simple as getting maybe only ten percent "mad" with other drivers in traffic this morning brought about a reason for me not to remain focused. This little lack of focus had me go up and down the stairs a few times because I was not paying attention to what I needed to pay attention to, maybe the other drivers this morning had their own reasons for not paying attention as they drove and maybe they have a difficult time staying focused because of some other knock on effect in their own morning that led their thoughts to become confused. Again, this sounds pretty simple really. It is worth thinking about because if I can get confused about what a simple thing like forgetting to check what level I parked the car on, then it would be fair to say so could another person get confused for a second about which lane they needed to be in when they drove around the city this morning too. Could I have spared a "thought" for them this morning and saved myself the hassles of having to run back up and down to the parking garage?

But what about if they were to spare a thought for me this morning and drive more carefully? Yes, all possible too. Where does this kind of thinking come from to begin with, if in that simple example there of how a day can side shift momentarily based on a little thinking in our heads then where might the thought begin in the first place? The domino effect is easy to spot in a negative light and easy to say the bad driver was under pressure for some other reason which in turn brought about my delay in leaving the parking garage. Where might the happier positive domino effect come from?

It would have to start with ourselves really. We would have to not allow our thoughts run away with us for a split second just because we want to react to another driver, we might want to begin again and start the niceness all over. Remember now I am heading off to spoil myself a little for the day and why allow someone else's poor thoughts and decisions affect my day. For this reason and as a way to get back in line for the day, I hold the elevator door for an elderly couple as they are slow walkers and cannot run to catch it. This can begin again my thoughts on humanity and the nice of everybody and for me to hold that door is a more positive way for my day to go. I hope and will continue to hope that if I show courtesy to others in the world, I might receive some back too. My thoughts are back on track.

I walk out from that parking garage that seemed to have almost locked me in for eternity and the streets are buzzing. Wow so many people are going places and going there fast too. I side-step my way among them and off to the windows for a look here and there. I am back on track and feeling good. Why feeling good? I am feeling good because we all know when we are about to buy ourselves something it feels nice. Some call it retail therapy or something like that and some others suffer addictions to it. I feel good. My thoughts have been clear and focused about what my plan is for my day and I am now in the middle of carrying out this plan and the emotion is I am feeling good. Earlier was a little road rage which brought about a little lapse in focus and muddled me up a tiny bit, I lost track of where exactly I had parked? And my emotions were a little angry.

Clear thoughts, check.
Focused on plan, check.
Emotions feeling good, check.

Not a bad little recipe so far to the day. The little bump in the road and the back tracking to the car park were no big deal and it is working out for me again. I could have quite easily been in a completely different situation. Let's explore.

The driver who has cut across me now as I clearly have my signal on is nothing but an asshole. I am going to speed down in front of him and honk and if I can make it to the lights before him, I can cut him off and just sit at the light and not move. If he tries to go around me, I will pull out a little and I can screw up his day. Who does he think he is? Fuck him and his cut me off in traffic, I pull out from around him and honk and give him the finger, "fucking taxi driver" I yell at him and then I jam on the breaks right in front of him. Fuck this mother fucker who thinks they can fucking ruin my day and just carrying on, out there in the world, to drive like an asshole cutting anyone off whenever they want. I throw my hand out of my window in the air so to let him know all his honking behind me is not going to stop me and I will keep him blocked in as long as I can.

I have the day off and have nothing to do really. He swoops out past and gives me a look of disgust as he drives past so I race down to the next light over taking him and cut in in front of him again. This time I am going to sit here all the way through green and if he wants to move, he will have to hit me from behind to which I will get out and give him an opportunity to get a real beat down for himself. Yup this is the right way and fuck him. He goes to pull out around me and I swerve out a bit to block him more, there is another horn blowing from another car and then bang! Another car coming up the street has crashed into the taxi from behind. Traffic is all stalled and the taxi driver is out talking with the other driver. I can see in my rearview mirror the taxi driver speaking with the other driver and they are waving their hands about and the taxi man is pointing to my car. Fuck this, the light is green and off I go. I circle back and am back on track to go about my days shopping, only four blocks down the way a motorbike cop has signaled me from behind to pullover. He wants to know why I have left the scene of an accident. I tell him I heard the bang and it was behind me, so it didn't affect me. He tells me how the woman in the back of the taxi is pregnant and is on her way in an ambulance to hospital, three witnesses say I caused the accident by some kind of road rage incident and I will need to come to the station by way of escort for further investigations.

Oh shit!!!!!

I am feeling like shit and the troubles now are about to get a whole lot worse. I have witnesses against me and by getting all caught up in some stupid thought process of wanting to be right and drive mad and teach him a lesson, I have landed myself in some tricky hot water.

Thoughts of madness, check.

Lost focus, check.

Emotions, feel like shit, check.

Two simple ways in which my day can turn out just from how I decided to allow my thoughts run wild with me and cause all kinds of problems or the simple not allow it all to happen and end on track feeling good on the high street. What is in the example or the scenario? I let my head race and decided in a moment of complete madness to allow my thoughts take over my whole judgement and decision-making process, the result of this has been bad and shows me that in allowing these thoughts to take over cannot lead to anywhere good. Not allowing them to take over caused me a little tiny run up and down the stairs and left me holding the elevator for an elderly couple. I ended on the street going about my day all nice and calm and relaxed. This is the point I am getting to. All calm and relaxed and even performing nice gestures. One simple thought in my car in traffic and allowing that thought to make my decision for me can bring me to a nice day or a horrible day. How or what I decide to do about my thoughts can lead me to somewhere completely different in a matter of minutes.

Sounds a little far-fetched and too dramatic I hear you say, pregnant lady and car crash, too much already, perhaps? It can all happen as easily as that. When we let our thoughts take over our minds, we are opening the door to all possibilities and nothing is far-fetched when we decide to race through the streets in a fit of rage. Not all of us engage in rage or "road rage" and are a little more submissive in our way of driving. We do not let other drivers even bother us. Our thoughts stay focused on the task at hand much more easily and have no desires to race through lanes of traffic. Some of us, we don't even drive so we take the train to the city. Our thoughts are more about ourselves and our position in the world.

So, let's say I take the train to the city. I allow the other people to board ahead of me and I spend my journey standing by the doorways. I watch as people get on and off and I look around a little bit, I notice everybody, but nobody notices me. I didn't get someone to offer me the hand gesture of "please go ahead". I spend the journey just thinking to myself. How come they do not notice me? What would happen if I were just to disappear? Would anyone really notice? I wanted to feel better about myself and head to the city to buy myself something nice because I spend so much time stuck in my thoughts and my own depression that it has taken everything, well a little effort anyway just to make a day for myself and head to the city. Who really cares if I sit for my journey? I am just me. I spend my time and a lot of it in my thoughts and only in my thoughts. My feelings are low most of the time and it is just life, like what is the big deal? So, who would really care if I were to go missing, or who or why does it even matter that I buy some nice clothes? Thoughts alright, just thoughts. I have chosen to spend my day on myself and take a little care of myself, mostly because people have said this would be the best thing, I could do for me. Maybe they recognize my depression and only advise me to buy myself something nice just so that I can feel good about myself, who really knows.

If I wanted to be nice to myself and I want to really take some control over how I feel and what I might do with all these thoughts that seem to keep me down, is perhaps to just be nice to myself. Take the time at the train station to be first to board the train and ensure myself a comfortable seat for my little journey into the city. Maybe someone else can do the standing for a change. Even better for me to make sure and grab a seat by the window where I can fall into dreams in my day as I see the fields and the ocean stream past my window. The only people I need notice are those reflections in the window that come and go as the scenery behind turns from dark to lighter. Gazing out the window and seeing the nature around me on my journey could be enough to lift up my spirit. Such a little thing as taking care of myself or putting myself first for a change could bring about a nicer day, how about that? I have kind of just amazed myself at the idea of not being the super submissive and allowing others to push past me or even push ahead of me and all this can change my day and bring about a nicer feeling just by how I have boarded the train. Of course, there is no need to be rude in boarding the train and no need to push anyone to the side, I can remain respectful to all around me and still take care of myself first.

Staring out the window of the train allows my mind to float a little with the birds that I see in the distance and how the green of the fields brightens my vision, I do not even have a thought of who or what noticed me as I am noticing everything. What a simple exercise to begin a journey and a day out to the city in a brighter mood. Maybe and just maybe if I take the window seat more often my days can be nicer and feelings can sneak in to calm me, calm me as I feel my way through a daydream on my train ride. I forget the ideas of who noticed me and I begin to see outside instead of stuck inside my own thoughts. I can take over my day by not going deeper into myself in a depression and allow the day to fill me up a little brighter by the view I have from the window seat.

Such a simple thing is that train ride and how different it can be by where I stand or sit, just like the car parking, it is how I think and act that can keep my mind racing or depressed. If we stay in our mind or allow our mind to take us over, we are entering into a place or a space that can bring us down, allowing ourselves to hurt our own life. It is not caused by the other people on the train and is not caused by the taxi driver who cut me off. It is "I" or "we" that can take some power over how we think and then this can result in how we feel. We have the built-in mechanisms inside of ourselves to actually allow our day to be a chaotic mess of road rage or a depressed state of "nobody notices me". We can choose to be calm in the traffic and get to where we want to be and fill our body up with a nice feeling, just like when I got to the street and was ready to shop my day away and also just as I gazed out of the window on the train and saw the beauty of the world. I allowed myself and my body to be filled with nice! Just by putting myself first and taking my place in the seat by the window. These are a couple of examples and very simple examples to help you see how I see. A little bit of how it does not take much to change how our day can go and really the ability we have inside of ourselves to think ourselves into a very negative position in our minds. We possess the ability to make room for ourselves in the world without hurting anybody and most importantly we can allow our feelings to flow just as easily as we can allow our minds to race. We can let our thoughts and feelings flow together and enjoy both of them, all we need to do is stay clear to ourselves about what our day entails and not allow the thoughts to take over. Simple really and so simple there are a lot of us that do not stop to think how we can accomplish this in our day, all by ourselves.

Simple moments of remaining focused on ourselves and on our day can help us steer a clear path and we can enjoy our day. We can feel good. Thinking and remaining deep in ourselves can leave us in hot water of chaos or feeling down. It is within our own ability to make this fabulous change and we reap the benefits.

Behaviour (Good or Bad?)

How can we or one of us or you, let's stick with we as it makes it nicer to feel like I am including you in my writing and I am included within your thoughts as you are reading. Now that we got that out of the way, how can we bring about our behavior? How do we behave is a mighty question all on its own, although there are variables too? How do we behave in any given situation would be one such variable that could be mentioned? Again, it takes examples and some thoughts on ideas of what is our behaviour and when is our behaviour.

I can behave like an altar boy and walk around with my head and my posture so heavenly that I exude every ounce of what "godliness" perhaps would look like, if we knew what that might actually, be. I can slouch and hang my head as I go about my day and I may receive from the world exactly what I put out by my slouched presence, or we could hold ourselves upright and allow our presence be known that we are here and that we are open to all and any comments or interactions with an open mind and well, just an openness to our fellow humans. These kinds of things are what our posture or gait says to others about us. A good way to begin taking a little time with our behaviour. The world sees us not as we see ourselves but how they see us.

We can spend a lot of money on designer clothes and have a nice watch on our wrist or some very expensive shoes for example and this can help for us to give off a warm healthy image. There is absolutely nothing wrong with a positive and healthy image, this is great actually. What does come to mind though is how our image is a three second glance from someone and nothing more. How we carry ourselves in our posture may be absorbed by others around us much more than what our image is. Out there in the public our image is taken in by people in about three seconds yet our vibe and how we hold ourselves seems to be viewed by other human beings, like a sixth sense kind of thing. So, for this reason I would think that expensive clothing looks great and is good to feel comfortable in but are not the b all end all of anything really. We can be "dressed to the nines" as they say and still hold ourselves in such a way that no matter what arena we are in we can be left in the corner or by ourselves.

How we behave has a lot to do with how we carry ourselves in our bodies, how we stand and how we pose, how we enter a room or how we walk down the street. What does that have to do with behaviour? Yes, I heard you wondering.

Our behaviour can depend a lot on how we are received by others, almost like a candle for example or well, just the flame. We do not think about any chemical reactions when we look at a candle, some of us even begin to think of the candle as a symbol of peace and/or the thoughts of a loved one who has passed. But what is actually going on with a candle while it is doing its burning. I guess here is a good place to openly admit I am no science major or anything like that. A candle is burning and for the best of my knowledge there is a thing about oxygen being needed to keep the flame going. We do not see the oxygen as it mixes to make the flame, no.

We see a candle burning. When a candle is big and beautiful, we may notice it, but it is the flame that we see first and most often we recognize and enjoy how it looks and how it moves or flickers. The little candle we do not notice as much, but we can still see the flame. We are just like the candle as when we are among other people there is nobody walking around saying to themselves "oh my, look how much air that person is breathing" or " I wonder how much oxygen is attaching itself to each red blood cell within that person as they walk across the room, hmmmm?" No! Just like the candle it is the flame they notice, the flame within us. If we carry ourselves well, well-meaning upright and with great posture, people will probably notice us just like the big ornate candle, however it is, or it can be how we behave that allows others to see our flame. There are no burning flames coming out of us, I know, it is how we behave that is our flame.   Like have you ever just met someone for the first time and you remember nothing about what they were wearing or when they came in the room or anything like that as they were not striking in their clothing or anything special but you just turned to your friends sometime after an evening and said, "wow there is something about that person, I just like". It is almost like we all have that sixth sense inside ourselves, some will call it instinct and others will call it the "mind's eye" but we all ooze out certain auras and vibes basically to each other all of the time. I will never remember anyone for what exactly they looked like on the outside to be honest with you, however I will always remember how I felt around somebody more than likely due to how they oozed out their flame in my surroundings. Weird isn't it? How someone's mere presence can bring about a feeling within us, this does not necessarily mean it is a good or bad feeling, just a feeling. There are some people I have heard say "aw fuck! here comes so and so, I hate this fucker" harsh words I know but I have heard them said. So in that case it would have to be that some people get a bad feeling from some people and on the opposite end of things I have also heard someone say "I am so glad they are here as I get great vibes when they are around" this would mean there is a good feeling registering with that person when xyz person is around. So, it can be a good or bad feeling when someone's presence is felt.

Behaviour I have been told once or twice before that there are a couple of types of behaviour in all of us. There are the basic instincts within us which carry some instincts just like it says, we have an instinctive way of behaving because we are by design made to survive and so we act certain ways to allow ourselves to try and be as comfortable as possible in any given place, time or situation. Our simple basic instinct to survive will make us sit when we are tired and push past another person to try and get first in a line if we are hungry and the line is for food. We will cross a street if we feel some form of danger may be ahead of us or change seat on the bus if we are feeling uncomfortable by the person sitting next to us. These would be some very simple instinctive kind of ways to behave and we do have many more of them but just a few to mention. We also are supposed to have these other behaviours that are not from our animalistic instinctive side and they are called learned behaviours. These are ways in which we learned to behave by watching others. From as little as a few weeks old when our little baby eyes could focus, we began watching people around us. We started paying attention with our minds eye and watched how others around us behave and we started to copy them. I have to admit that this kind of stuff amazes me really, cause how, before we could ever speak or read or write or knew anything about any academics or anything, did we know to pay attention and learn? Learned behaviours come from instinctive behaviour, amazing! We knew to survive out in this world we needed to watch others and learn. Our basic instinct to survive has brought about within ourselves to learn from others and watch closely how others act and behave and we see what it does for them and so we begin to copy them a little bit and learn how to get what we need. Yes, these early learnings can be quite simply a tantrum to get food. Our instinct says we need to eat and so as a young baby we cry to let others know we need food. As we might watch and learn from an older sibling that is a little expert at crying and tantrum type stuff, so we learn how we might get the food we want too. So, we have learned how to behave before we even knew how to walk. As early as a toddler we were learning how to behave.

What constitutes good behaviour? Sounds like something that could be mentioned alongside a parole hearing or something, let out of jail early for good behaviour. This is not what I am talking about though. I am talking about how we all behave from day to day and what makes any of us different from each other. The majority of us know or are aware of what they once called "good manners" and "etiquette" so we probably follow along the lines of these even if only just barely, we do behave somewhat civilized at the best of times. So why call it good behaviour, why not call it normal or everyday behaviour? We look for reward for this good behaviour, funny that but yes just how the parolee seeks some reduced time from his prison sentence for his good behaviour as his reward for this, we too have learned from a very young age that if we behave correctly or carry ourselves with "good behaviour" we get rewarded in some way and so from as young as toddler age we have been learning this, (learned behaviour) we learned it.

What reward do we seek as we are now adults and so we are not looking for an extra cookie or to have a little stay up late time to watch movies as perhaps we once did as children. What reward do we seek now? If we are good now in our adult lives what rewards can be sought after by us for conducting our daily lives in a manner of good behaviour? To be left alone and allowed to be our selves perhaps would be a decent enough reward. To be promoted at work or to gain confidence and trust in our relationships with our partners and grow as individuals would be a couple of possible rewards and reasons why we act and maintain a good behaviour record in our lives. The prison inmate has his reasons, very simply for his good behaviour, he wants to get out of prison early, that is quite understandable. We may actually be God fearing people and live a certain way so as to receive our reward in the next life in heaven and we continue our daily life to do good and act well and behave according to laws and rules of a Bible, for the reason of seeking our reward. We may just have learned from our toddler age that the easiest way to a happier life is to be good and behave well. There is of course the idea that through process of elimination that we have learned that it has been by crossing off the results of bad behaviour that has led us to understand how terrible things can be when we behave badly that has led us to understand how to achieve what we wish to achieve is best done by not behaving badly.

Examples are bursting all over my mind of how to explain good behaviour versus bad and what the results of each bring about. You probably have plenty of your own ideas too of a time when you experienced something in life that brought you some sort of "not the desired results" so we learn again by weighing up the good versus the bad of the results of times when we have behaved good and times when we have behaved badly and slowly but surely we figure out a path to walk along that allows us to be ourselves firstly and then after, that allows us some joy in our daily lives. Like let's be honest, if we are an ass to people, we probably don't get too far with them and even though we are not in a game of trying to get far with people we do prefer to get along with most folks most of the time.

Some of us may well have grown up in a family home where our poor behaviour was rewarded and good behaviour meant nothing or was never recognized so our learning curve was, do bad to get results and doing good was already expected but never acknowledged and so for this we may have come a long way in life to never actually understand the whole, how we behave concept or meanings.

Some of us out there in the big bad world may only have ever achieved by behaving badly and so we may never know what it is like to have the simplicity of do good equals rewarding times. Some of us may actually have done good for a very long time and behaved quite well only to bump into another who has only learned to behave badly and so we feel like we get shit on for doing good all the time and keep finding these or those who behave poorly. Some of the even stranger things we can come across in our daily lives can be where we believe we are doing right in our words and actions on any given day and we might just have never actually heard our own point of view as how we express it or how it is perceived by others. We go along with our good posture and our nice clothes and present ourselves in our attitudes quite well and never give thought of how do we actually behave? We do not understand why it is that we get into arguments with people or why our friend lists are quite few and we do not understand why no matter how fun a general get together may be, we find ourselves alone or feel out of place. Maybe and I am saying maybe on purpose here, maybe we are not received or perceived in the same light like how we view it in our own mind, maybe others think we behave badly by how they have went through their learning of behaviour and so it is not by our own standards that we are understood. We think we deliver simple words from our mouth and that our hand gestures and body language are polite and normal, though those around us may find us offensive or rude and consider us to be ill mannered or impolite. For this concept alone it definitely would make sense that life is a constant tight rope balancing act of how and what to be, then add in the when and where variables and now things start to make a little sense of why some find it more difficult than others. These ideas of how to behave really are just some ideas and to put more simply let's take a look step by step.

Appearance;

*Look well and maintain some good hygiene.

*Dress smart and be clean.

*Smile and the world smiles right back.

Posture;

*Hold your head high, chin up to look people straight in the face.

*Carry shoulders straight and walk as tall as is possible without dominating the crowd.

Smile and the world smiles right back.

Behaviour;

*Be receptive to others and mannerly.

*Do good and seek no reward.

Smile and the world smiles right back.

Attitude;

*Be bright and positive to allow for best reception.

*Be understanding to the needs of others as we do not know how others may have learned their behaviour.

Smile and the world smiles right back.

All of the above I have finished with, "smile to the world" mentioned as it is through this that I have learned that it is only possible to find our own level of comfort amongst our equal fellow human beings, that a smile can be contagious and when one person does it, yes it can spread like a wildfire.

What do you want from your life? To go around all full of cheer and be so bright and optimistic that one day life hits you like a ton of bricks and all the hateful nasty people show up all at once to bring us down so far that we cannot climb up and out of it? No, I did not think so. A balance of how we present ourselves coupled with some understanding of how our own ideas of how and in what way we should behave, to not only gain us some reward but perhaps to offer reward to others too. Yes, life is selfish, and it is correct to be on the lookout for yourself at all times yet perhaps there is another less fortunate than you. There is the possibility that another human right in front of your very own eyes may not find things quite so easily and they may have never been rewarded for their own good behaviour, they may have been beaten as a child and never understood or never learned as you did and so when you have a wonderful idea of how you carry yourself and how you present yourself and even of how you behave, maybe another did not ever understand what you do. Someone else may never have an understanding of how you perceive things and another human being may never have even had a thought the same as you have. For these reasons a massive piece of how to behave within our society of today is to carry yourself with a smile. The smile will be the best piece of dress you can wear on any given day and in any given situation. A smile can be contagious, so no matter how someone else around you may have grown up or how they may have learned their own behaviour, a smile can do so much more for them than it can for you and this would have to be considered the nicest way to behave of all.

As I had mentioned a little earlier, the idea of how we ooze out our own attitudes and personas and who we are deep inside by saying nothing and just being. This is something that not even the most expensive clothes can hide nor do we know how we look to the mind's eye of another and we can speak so loudly to them by our attitude and our behaviour that we didn't even need to speak a word. This is amazing, some call them chakras and lights and energies between humans that we just can sense each other. Others will call them vibes, I like to think of our sixth sense as the mind's eye, the ability we have to know something without very much thought at all.

If we know who we are inside of ourselves then we can know how it is that we come across to others and we probably know how to behave in all and any situations we find ourselves in. Some important things to note might just be, how we hold ourselves in our own esteem. If we love ourselves then we will ooze love to another's senses, and they will vibe off of that and feel good around us. If we ooze our self-pity and self-loathing all the fancy jewelry will never hide it. Yet how can we behave in a way to fool someone or anyone and behave like an actor to give off a different vibe? We just cannot. It really is how we conduct ourselves that another picks up on and this cannot be hidden. If we are finding out about ourselves and loving ourselves then we can begin to see what others see about us and we then can build some strengths to be a pure person from inside to outside, so really there would never be a need to act in any way that is not of our true self. Best to begin to know our own lives better before we worry about what anyone might think of us and for this reason our behaviour does begin with how we treat ourselves on the inside.

We can think we are a particular person or have a particular way in how we behave and we may feel we are a mind full of knowledge on how to act right and behave well when really, we lack the knowledge of our self. We do not know ourselves on the inside and so how can we love ourselves truly? We deserve a true loving feeling for ourselves regularly and we deserve to be not only looking good but also feeling good, it is these feelings that will speak volumes to others, also present are senses and vibes that will carry us through an array of situations where it will never matter how we behave because our own true being will do all the talking for us.

Imagine just for a moment that all these types of things are going on without ever speaking to another or ever even looking someone in the eye yet. Another human being can sense all these things about us just by being in our presence, if we are involved with our own presence then we know. A good question to our self might just be.

Who am I?

This is of course something different for each of us to ponder over many times throughout our lives as we do change slightly through time and our behaviour can display to people around us exactly how in touch with our own self inside that we really are.

Let's say we were to go for a job interview. The scenario is twofold, first off, we really want the job and we need some income these days so it is important that we make a good impression and show the interviewer that we are a very good candidate and full of knowledge about the company where we are applying to. We want to let them know we want the job but we do not want to seem too needy or nervous and we just want to get the job. And so, we enter the interview room in very respectful attire, new suit and look like we are a real go getter in business. We walk in and great each person with a handshake, all introductions over and the interview panel begin some basic questioning, light and normal stuff, how they have reviewed our application and they ask us how we see our self as being an asset to the company? This is where we rattle off some of the memorized stuff we have brushed up on about their company and we go a little further to explain what we can bring to table. We continue to maintain eye contact all around the table and display a very mannerly and well-behaved person indeed. We feel we are owning the interviewers and as we walk out, there are some more handshakes and some smiles from them to us and all round, we feel confident. Our interview technique we feel has worked and they seemed happy.

A little time passed by and we have not heard anything back from the company we were applying to. We call them up and they inform us the position has been filled and we did not get the job. We ask if we may know the reason why and the person on the other end of the phone gives a standard reply, "it says here that you were overqualified for the job". This is difficult for us to understand, we did everything textbook in the interview and we were very good with our knowledge and communication with the interviewers, this really makes no sense to us and we really wanted the job. What we probably forget to take into consideration is that a person doing an interview is a very trained eye type of person and not only are they in touch with perceptions and realities as they see them but their minds eye is very alert too. They saw us in a smart dress for the interview and they heard us speak very highly and well educated about the position we were applying for. They even maintained the good cheer laughing and great conversation with us all the way to the elevator too. What went wrong?

We did not fool them and they knew from the moment we walked through the door that we were performing and going through the motions. They believed immediately that we were so well dressed that we didn't seem to need the position and our knowledge was a bit above theirs for the position of the job in the first place. They saw us to be affording nice clothes carrying ourselves well and so educated on the position that we were applying for that they didn't really see a need for us to have the job and so they decided against us. We carried ourselves like a manual for a robot and did a textbook great interview, what we failed to do was be real and behave accordingly. We did not show our true self to them and the vibes were conflicting. We needed the job and we didn't let them know that. We were not being truthful and did not allow our look and our actions and our speech all match. The vibe they got was different to our image and the speak they got from us, though great, it was again not matching of our inner self. They saw this or sensed it and so we lose out on the job.

How about we run the same interview in a different way. We show up on time and nicely dressed, we converse to the interviewers how much we know about the position, but we let some of our true self out. We behave exactly how a person who wants a job is and that is usually totally desperate but due to being a true to ourselves kind of person, our speak to the interviewers may sound something like this., " In all honesty I can probably do the job with my eyes closed and am definitely an over qualified type person, however I do need the job and it is something that would really make me happy. I have practiced and memorized much about the position, but the truth is I am so willing to learn that I am almost nervous for the interview today. I hope I am not coming across conceited or in any way like a big head about working for your company.

I am just an emotional person and it helps me stay grounded if I share with you how I actually feel rather than some rehearsed "speech"

Boom you got the job this time. And why? Because your vibe and your presence complimented exactly how you looked and spoke. There was no practiced way it should be. It was just you being you in a very nice and human way. Other humans recognize humans. So, when a picture on a menu looks delicious and then when you order it and eat it, it is delicious and all aspects match in sync, then this is a success. All because we can portray to others in how we are on the inside as well as the outside and the two are not conflicting, then this is a successful way to carry ourselves and how to act and speak alongside how to behave, all by just being ourselves.

It makes me wonder a lot of the time and might even make you wonder too. All that about an interview is an example to take a little peek at what being in touch with ourselves and being able to communicate it to the outside world can actually do for us. When you are "on" you are on and people get great vibes from this. Sometimes even people will say things like "I don't know what they have but I want some of it". This kind of knowing ourselves on the inside and allowing it out to the outside world can be so productive and help us in many areas of life that why would we not focus a little time on it and get to know how to love ourselves from the inside. Spend some time getting to know how we are perceived and what all our learned behaviours have thought us and how we act accordingly. Something so simple as getting a new job can all go quite easily and successfully by just knowing ourselves. Makes me want to work on myself even more too, don't you?

Being polite all of the time to everybody we meet is such a wonderful concept and the ideal world would of course be somewhat of "the perfect place" should we all wander around spewing love a good cheer to everybody, it does not happen and we are human. Being human seems to have its own drawbacks by way of we all have some few character defects here and there and that is just one simple fact of life. Defects, sounds like a seconds run of a factory product that we buy at a warehouse sale or something "oh I forgot and cheaper cause they had some little defects, they are factory seconds". Not in the case of all humans, we would not be right or balanced if we did not have a few defects here and there. Anyone could argue the point that it can be easy to spot a person's character flaws or see their defects a mile away, but can we really go deep into the issue and find defects in ourselves?

What are the things we do not like about ourselves? It has been said to me only about a million times by many different types of people, "the things we do not like about another person are really the things we do not like about ourselves" What?????, Yup it is said that when we get that feeling about someone and we think to ourselves how we just "hate it" when they do _____.

Yup whatever that is, is something we hate within ourselves, well, dislike in ourselves. Hate is such a tough word to use for anything really, we are better off to consider it that we dislike these things in another is a reflection of something we dislike within ourselves.

Through our dislike of another or our self for that matter we will act accordingly around some people and this will develop in to how we act and behave all of the time in any such situation. We are like robots or slaves to ourselves really. If we do not like something within ourselves, we find a way to convince ourselves it is the other person and how they act so childish is what just presses our buttons and we cannot stand it. We just cannot be around that person when they act in that way. So we alter our course to avoid them or fake a reason not to be around them and that would seem quite simple really, we could change our whole day around just to avoid a "type of person" when we know there is something about their defect that we just do not like. It does not mean we do not like the person, we just don't like some or a little bit of how they are or how they act/behave. If it is true that it is a reflection of ourselves and it is how they behave that we do not like because it is something, we dislike about ourselves on the inside then we are enslaving ourselves and we are avoiding our own self. The example being the person who acts childish and we just cannot stand it, sometimes it is that we on the inside are also very childish and we cannot allow ourselves to be the childish person that we are, we do not like how this other person can just so freely be themselves and let their childishness out. So, we in our mind consider them to be annoying and we do not like it, when there is a very good chance, we are jealous of their ability to just be themselves and allow their true self out. We will behave in any amount of ways to hide our true self on the inside and not allow our inside out to the world. We will sidestep and mumble or say nothing in situations because we cannot just freely be ourselves. This is the piece I was saying is making us a slave to ourselves. It takes a lot of work for someone to keep it all in and just speak to themselves in their mind more than they express and let themselves out in the world. There are the things or ways in how others behave that we can allow to affect our own lives. Something someone else does that can keep our own minds racing.

We do have the ability to begin to get to know ourselves and our own defects and work through some of them to become a whole and happy person. It is then that our own behavior will always tell our own story to others in the world. Our own behavior can speak so much about us in life that it only stands to reason that we keep a little bit of focus around ourselves most of the time. Worrying about others or thinking of things we do not like in others has no bearing on how we conduct ourselves.

EFFECTS

So, from how we have learned to behave and our ability to allow our inside thoughts and feelings just flow, what are the effects these things can take on our life? Where do we draw from within ourselves to become the person we are? Not just the person that we think we are but the person everybody sees and gets to know. Some will dislike the person that we are and we can chalk that down to some piece inside of themselves that they dislike and others will like us all the way. Some will even love us to a point of they, "like us a lot", every inch of our being.

What or how have, what we have learned from being a toddler up until now that makes us the person that the everyday world sees? How much of ourselves do we allow the rest of the world to see? To what affect do we effect the people around us and more to the point what effect has our skill set of hiding certain pieces of our being from the world, what effect has it had? Have we allowed our self to become somebody that we are not? Have we developed some, now very deep routed skills at hiding inside that we do not know how to undo or change our ways and habits? These are all very worthy questions and no reason for us to go into very deep territory at all. We can take a look at what we do and how we do it and see what are our own skill sets? Some of us, l, well to be honest it is my belief that most of us are sensitive in many areas of our lives and our emotions are a fountain of, well, skittles really. Yeah skittles, why not? Or starburst for those who do not know skittles (rainbow candy assortment) the rainbow colours representing all the different emotions inside of us and at any time, any other colour can just come gushing out of us. These feelings we experience have no real warning signs and can pop up from anywhere, usually of course there is some sort of stimulant that can trigger a feeling, so let's say a situation in front of us on any given day and an emotion can be felt. More often than not if we are in our trusted network of friends or very close family, we may just allow our emotions to flow and enjoy the time of it. Enjoy the time of it meaning we feel it all the way, not necessarily a joyful feeling or anything but we can let our guard down and be ourselves in a trusted circle of close people. Now, give us a situation of similar strength to muster up some emotional occurrence and we are among some not so close friends or a work gathering of some sorts and we might not, let the emotion flow as naturally as we would have done among our tight knit entrusted friendship circle. Why would we hide ourselves among those who do not know us so well? Perhaps there are too many reasons for this.

We do not feel safe nor are we comfortable being emotional around our work colleagues, such soft natured stuff has no place in the workplace and allowing our guard to drop in a place of business might be the worst thing we could ever do, well it seems we may just have conditioned ourselves this way at least. Then if that is the case where do these few lines of conversation come from?

"Oh, they are such a lovely person, once you get to know them"

Or

"When I met them first, I thought they were so stuck up it is not even funny, but now that we have been together so long, trust me this person is amazing"

A couple of simple lines we may have heard once or more in our lifetimes when speaking of another person. What do they speak when they speak of you? Now that's a good question. Let us leave that one alone for a while as we could go off on a multitude of tangents on that one for sure. So, what has been the effect on ourselves of holding the true self on the inside and what damage or for want of a better term what hard fastened set of rules have we placed upon ourselves when it comes to our own life?

What effect has all of our years brought about to us? There are many of us who can see the gold dress in the internet post that floated around for a while and there are also many of us who can hear the word "Yanny" on that other viral post that did the rounds. Some of us do see things the same and some of us do hear things the same also, that is a relief. Please do not be paranoid when I say some of us keep it all hidden inside as I am not talking directly about you right now, there are many of us just like the gold or blue dress and that, there are many of us who have kept it all hidden inside for a very long time. It really is about taking a look at, what or how we have developed our own skills and how we have allowed others and situations take effect on our entire life. We can use a couple of examples again, like for example,

We were hit as a child when we got cheeky or bold in the presence of adults. We were but a child and we did not really know what we were saying, or we didn't understand what being cheeky to our elders really meant and so we received a slap on the ass or sometimes maybe some of us received worse. There was a beating maybe waiting for us at home for some trouble we had gotten in to at school. Whatever our bad behaviour was, it was our parent's way to make an attempt to teach us right from wrong and a punishment was to get hit. That in itself is rather nasty to think of and if you are reading this right here at this moment, please accept my deepest sympathies if you were indeed beaten in any way as a child. I do not agree with it and feel horrible for any who have had to suffer under the hands of another.

For this example, we may have shut ourselves down as a person. We want to say things and we like that we form opinions inside of our own beings but at an early age in life we have been conditioned to say nothing unless contributing something positive or even worse we have developed a set of skills for self that we do not comment unless we are asked, which may have stemmed from receiving punishments as a child for speaking out. Again, as a child we did not know if we were being rude or not. We just said what we thought and we did not seek any need to feel justified to do so. This is probably why children are so brutally honest and speak a lot of truth as they have not been conditioned in any way by society yet. The feelings inside of them come out funny but are so pure and so for this reason children are so honest. As an adult it might be worth thinking about being a child again sometimes and just letting the inner us out in the world as we know the difference now of what is rude and what is not and another adult is not going to lift their hand to us just because we voice an opinion. The satisfaction part is that we feel something inside and we convey it to the world around us. How hard can that be?

It is not our duty to the world or any of the people around us that we should keep it all in. In order to be in a sense of being genuine and sincere we must make attempts and efforts to be who we are on the inside on the outside too. Connecting the two worlds can bring about so much relief to ourselves that we begin to actually flourish in our own life. Anyone who wishes to quieten us or wished that we maintain our quiet inner self in check, well it is a possibility and only a possibility that such people are not "our peeps", and so do not really fit into our life in the first place. We cannot change any people to accept us for who we are and many may find us hard to deal with on any given day. The most important factor of being our self is that we are accepted by our peers and any relationships we are in do not come with a price tag of staying mute or keeping our emotional self, locked up or only permissible when granted permission by others. Nope we are not going for that at all.

As a child who was told to, "be quite", well that was then and we did not know how to speak clearly our mind and our emotions but now we are adults. We know how to speak and we can see the full value in maintaining a balance between the inside world of us and the outside world in which we live. Having these two worlds balanced allows us to let our inner child out to the world and in some cases, we have had them locked away for quite too many years now, so it is about time to go for that balance. The effect on our own personal being and our own emotional health can receive some massive steps of progress by bringing together the who we are and the who the rest of the world thinks we are. It is only by allowing ourselves to share with others about our thoughts and our feelings can the rest of society actually get to know us completely. Should anyone wish to judge us for that then so be it, it is them that are doing the judging and not us. It is only when those who judge us get to understand themselves will they realize that their error has been just that, to judge.

The other example would be of course the child who learned to not keep their peace around their parents but those who developed skills to always say what the adults wanted to hear and received praise for confirming their parent's belief system. In one sense it felt great to be allowed to speak freely but in the other it has been that we did not speak our own mind, nor did we discuss our direct feelings. We were however never hit or anything like that, we even received praise for being so good at expressing ourselves, of course as long as that opinion of ours was along the same lines of thinking as our parents.

In this example, we can highlight how some of us have developed from our early years into maybe a people pleaser or a person who really likes the approval we got from our parents thus leading us sometimes in to stranger relationships of where we are looking for praises rather than any validity or value. If we learned quickly as a child to speak exactly what was being sought by the adults around us, then we have perfected the art of pleasing people and seeking all the praise possible for being so outspoken and so well at it too. The puzzled piece would be taking a look at an imaginable scenario where what we have learned as children has developed inside of us for our entire life and is very much a part of who we are now. Although it is not the who we are as perhaps how we see it ourselves. It is the world around us who see us in one particular light or another, but we are just us. We do nothing different nor do we make attempts to be something that we feel we are not. So where is this miscommunication coming from?

A scenario of course.

As a child we always spoke to our father about sports and the game results and we even criticized the managers just at the perfect time when the game was on TV and our father's beloved team was losing. We knew to speak badly of the poor decision making by the coaches and we knew to speak with a gasp or too when our father's team did something ridiculous. We never really knew what we were saying anyway but we were granted the permission by our father's silence and were allowed time to continue talking. When it came to our mother, we always knew how to have a sympathetic ear as we saw her work tirelessly as a housewife. We didn't know the dynamic of family and we really had no clue how hard she was working but what we did know was that we got glances of endearment when we played along. These are skills we have learned from a very young age.

Translated to modern day, we perhaps never speak with any real meaning or purpose and we continue in both our work life and home life to play along. Say what gives us less grief or brings us less hardships. Are we developing relationships of any real value? What is the total effect on us as a person? On our own wellbeing and individuality, what is becoming of us as a person? Have we developed the personality type of a person who puts everyone else first? Their wellbeing, their needs or have we found that everyone comes to us to talk and spill all their problems to our ears. They tell us we give such great advice. Has anyone listened to your problems and have you sought another's advice? Hard to be the great listener and be a person who needs to offload and let out their inner self. Perhaps the world might not handle you is an excuse we can make to ourselves and so remains the true self inside, hidden.

These could be some of the simpler effects of how we have developed now that we have our own lives. What can we do about these items which have become like our second nature? What can we do? Is it possible to undo years upon years of how we have developed? What would allowing ourselves to begin again and retrain ourselves into being the same on the inside and the outside, actually do? Allow the world (well maybe not the entire world) but for the most part the people around us, allow what we deem as a weakness inside of ourselves or the person who we have always been hiding, allow that person out. Could this be disastrous, catastrophic even?

I want to hazard a guess and maybe share a tiny piece of info with you. It is not that bad and it will not be that bad. To retrain ourselves & to learn new habits can be a lot easier than you think.

Can you consider one day just walking outside of your comfort zone and beginning all over again?

Imagine to undo years upon years of ducking and diving with emotions. The countless times we retreated so deep inside of ourselves that even we had a hard time finding ourselves. And all for what? An idea that it might not be safe, there might be just horrible hurtful people ready to break us down and do what exactly? Tear us from limb to limb and an all-out cannibal festival might just break out all of a sudden in our very own office? Highly unlikely but there was always the chance and so we were lucky we never took it.

The effects of how we have developed is all possible to be changed and to retrain ourselves to new methods and begin to see security in people around us. If you do not feel secure with the people you have around you, then it might be a good idea to get new people around you. Makes a little sense at least doesn't it? When we live in fear of people around us, we can kind of do a couple of three things. Run for miles and separate our life from theirs forever. This might be a bit drastic if indeed the fear is only something, we have made up inside of ourselves just to cope. We can express our fears in a gentle and safe way, safe as it fits for us and see that perhaps our fears can be put at bay by the very people we did not fully trust, we may just learn really quickly that we were oh so wrong and it is indeed okay to begin allowing our inner self out.

Lastly, we can learn more about ourselves by how they respond to us. We can actually begin to see that for every time we are hiding and acting in any particular way, we can see from those around us that this is the person they have come to know and just continue on our charade, living forever in a world of not so true and not so self. I am beginning to think you might be catching on that I am slightly nudging you to give it a go.

Let the onion peel one thin layer at a time. Peeling onions can bring us all a few tears from time to time so be prepared of course. It probably is for this precise reason that the layers of the onion are the most precise metaphor ever used to explain how we begin to allow ourselves out to the world, peeling one little skinny layer at a time and of course tears can be very much part of peeling onions.

THE Mind, Body & Soul

What do we really know about ourselves? This is a question that can take us deeper than maybe we ever want to go. How does our mind actually work? So many questions when it comes to ourselves, like we are actually the most complex thing we will ever study or examine and I mean ever! What is up with that exactly? Our mind is probably, nah let's say definitely tougher to figure out than algorithms for creating Web scalping bots or crypto currency mining devices. What are they? Exactly, they are complicated internet stuff that many are making money off and we have very little understanding of them either. However, we could train ourselves to sit and learn them. We could train and take classes of figuring out how to write computer programs and begin making pennies from the Internet as a job. For this I doubt you feel you have the time or patience to begin learning all these computer programming techniques and so what is it about our mind as humans that is even more complex than these things?

My mind or your mind or the mind of the person sitting next to you, all different. Imagine that, all different and there we were thinking everyone thought like us and when people act certain ways and we say "oh I just don't understand you sometimes", forget about sometimes in that kind of a situation and it might be better to consider "I just don't understand you at all".

If we want to understand others and how their mind works, well it would be safe to say that we might want to have just an inkling of an idea of how we work ourselves before we think we can dive right in to thinking we can understand another person. Our mind, oh my, oh my, our mind! This thing that supposedly is inside of our brain somewhere and behind the face we love so much. When we peer into the mirror right before we head out with friends for a night on the town, right there behind our beautiful eyes is this thing they refer to as "mind". What is it? Oh, but sure it is how we think and what we use to explore ideas and have dreams and make notions about what and who we are, right? Imagine all that by telling ourselves how good we look while standing in front of the mirror on a Friday night.

Wouldn't it be possible to say our mind could be a bigger part of ourselves and not only the piece behind our skull, if we have watched enough CSI on TV then we always hear them going on about "swollen frontal lobe" and the "blunt force trauma" to it. Must mean that mind of ours in inside there somewhere.

Another question about our mind would be, where did this thing about "oh that's just your mind playing tricks on you", where does that come from? Are we to believe that the mind has A "mind of its own"? A lot of questions about this old mind malarkey alright. So, what is it is exactly?

I have even heard a few people say directly to me, "oh I want to take a peek into your mind", "see what it is you keep up in that mind of yours" so it is probably for those kinds of reasons I have settled on the idea that our mind is something that is "up" somewhere, the head seems like a good spot, somewhere in our brain or near it at least. Other people you may have heard making fun of someone and mention that "their brain is in their big toe". I think there is a possibility that our mind is part of us in our entirety, like it is made up of our emotional self and the neurons that shoot up and down our spine and through our nerve endings which we have all over our body too. Our mind is a kind of part of us that is not only in the head. So, the everything we feel and that meaning, feeling in an emotional sense and in a physical sense also. Let's think about an example, I am not sure how many of you have ever tried this but here is something we used to do as kids.

We would venture off in the fields around where we live and because there is a good mixture of farmland around us, we would often come across lands where they kept livestock animals of one kind or another. Could be horses or cows or even sheep, anyway the point is there were many places where electric fencing was in use, it is something farmers use to keep the animals in a designated field or an area. When we would come to this electrical fencing stuff, we all knew it would give you a shock if you touched it and often times, we dared each other to touch it. One could say right now here, "what was going on in your minds?" would be a very apt placing of the question. We had nothing better to do. So, we would build ourselves up to touch the wire, as we did the buildup, a ton of fear or some kind of scaredness would come over us and we would continue the buildup and reach out a hand to grab the wire. Always pausing and just slowly getting closer to the wire, we knew an electric shock was coming and because an electric fence operates on a pulse type of current the shock may have already passed along the fence and maybe for a split second there was nothing going to happen. So, we grab a little tighter and then CLICK it goes. The shock rivets through us from fingertips to shoulders and ass and ankles, the lot. So, what is the whole thing of our mind. What was in our mind alright when we were touching these electric fences. Let's think about it.

The experience was very much full of emotions, we were scared and afraid to show it among our friends, we were nervous which was obvious by how we moved our hand so slowly and kept pulling it back a few times, and our mind was telling us not to be afraid and just do it. When we got the shock, we jolted and our whole entire body felt the electric shock, we lost our mind for a milli second due to pain and really it was only a millisecond. The point being I guess, that was an experience where we had all kinds of parts of our body involved and all kinds of emotional stuff and the thoughts too. This could make a case that our mind is through our entire body and not just some little area up in our head. It is possible to say that obviously the experience of touching an electric fence is a tad more than everyday kind of stuff, but it is a highlight of how the mind, our mind can be a culmination of all parts of us. Not just a piece of something in our heads. To just note we did venture around the fields many times but only the time when it was like a dare or a big thing that we had to stand and brace ourselves for touching the wire was it such a heightened experience. There were many times when we might have jumped over such a fence or stooped under it along our trek to any other adventure and the shock may have hit but was never the big ouch and awe of the time when we were completely focused on it and all our friends were silent and waiting and daring us. I have to believe the concentration time was the heightened experience because my mind was focused on it.

This is another possibility to dig much deeper for many examples and the basic reason I wanted to share this one with you is to give a focal point to our mind and our experiences of how we may or may not actually experience things with our mind and where is or what is our mind? Using this example, it is clear to me that when we focus on something and we take a little time with it and we give a "thing" time and emotion and thought then the experience is heightened. Many times, in any given day of our lives we experience a ton of stuff and not all of it seems like a great new high in life. We walk into a supermarket and do our weekly grocery shopping, no big deal really. We sit on a bus or a train for our daily commute and again no real big deal. Why could this be? Perhaps because we had no build up to these daily tasks or we never gave some focus to them. We are not emotionally involved with our daily commute or the errands we run from day to day, though when we pause and give time to something of a negative nature and we begin to allow our mind to consider it, perhaps something someone had said to us earlier about someone talking behind our back about us. We know we will be heading out later to a get together, meeting of some sort and we will be seeing this person who it has been reported to us was talking about us behind our backs and now in this situation we are giving it time in our mind, some emotions are occurring and we will go to that meeting with a heightened feeling about the whole thing. So, when we give something time in our mind, just a thought or two it changes the way we see it, the way in which we feel it and the experience becomes a lot more than just a quick dash around the grocery store, or our mundane commute. Why so? Because we gave it a little time and a little thought. We have the ability to completely ignore most of what we experience in any given day and we tend to allow our mind give time to negatives and any situation that might allow us to run off with an idea and give it legs to run riot in our very own mind. And to keep in mind (very much intended) that it is when we involve our feelings and sometimes have physical feelings too like an impact physically that we completely change how we think and feel about anything, this opens up a whole new idea to me that our mind is very much part of our entire aura and is not just the brain piece of us.

I have heard many times that if we focus on it (anything) then it can become, like the self-fulfilling prophecies and the likes. There is a book that has been doing the rounds called "the secret" where it would suggest that we can manifest anything we wish and if we want a situation to occur, we can make it occur. There are like thousands of philosophies that will go back and forth on the subject and to go down that road here might mean we need a lot more paper for this book. To not allow us to run wild on the concept or any one philosophy of its kind let's just keep it a touch simpler and stick with some ideas of our own body and what our mind is to it and what effect we can bring about for ourselves. What manifestations do we bring about for ourselves regularly and of course remembering that our mind may very well be a whole part of our aura so our feelings both physical and emotional all play a part.

The classic has to be how we have the feeling of being tired, sometimes we will say "I feel exhausted". This leads us to be lazy kind of, heading for our bed and yawning. We may say to our partner "oh don't ask me, I am too tired to think". This sounds quite silly really because if we were too tired to think how would we navigate our way upstairs or to our bedroom? So maybe we are actually just saying, I am too tired to get involved emotionally, physically and mentally in the topic or questions. This also would be a good way to consider that our thinking can operate on kind of an auto pilot type setting to help us get up those stairs and in to bed but our mind does not wish to be disturbed as we feel exhausted. Again, suggesting that our mind is more than just what is going on in our brain and our line of thoughts or thinking. When we say we feel exhausted, do we really mean the words, or do we just use it because it is what we understand to express our feeling of tiredness? I believe it is a way to express how we are not willing to engage our mind any more for the day and sleep time is needed.

So back to how we use our mind and how we may or have been trained within our society to pay attention to negatives. There is a real "thing" that society is responsible for and that is the use of negatives and how we as humans seem to crave them more and more. It is not any one individuals' fault that they have become depressed or that they crave or live to create negativity. Our societies around us have been finding them more and more acceptable and we just grew up in these such societies, so we never knew any different. It is our mind that will tell us that something is good or bad for us, if we are paying attention, that is.

We will allow and accept a certain amount of abuse in our life from even our friends and we do not think any differently about it as it is a widely acceptable form of behavior among our society. Abuse sounds a harsh word and we might even now start thinking of this word & stray off a little bit in our mind and think of how "not me I have never been abused" that would be what I would call "extreme abuse" is what you may be thinking of. The abuse I am referring to is the simple slagging each other amongst friends. "taking the piss" or "taking the mick" with each other. These are forms of negative activities that because we have become used to our friends calling us fat or stupid that we never think anything other than it is normal. These are simple examples to use about forms of negative games we play while growing up and they become part of what we consider normal as they have never been of any extreme nature to where we were severely bullied or anything of that nature. What this acceptable tolerance and normalization is doing is laying a foundation or pathway for us in our life that we allow the negatives into our mind. This is where they will live forever. Also remembering that I am saying our mind is a place that is more than just our brain. So, the acceptability of negative slurs or slanders have become normal to us and we have built a certain tolerance to them, some might call that "having thick skin".

We continue in life and never really consider or notice any of these things because it is going on all around us and society has accepted certain negatives to be permitted. The result is, any one person may develop a complex inside of themselves and some even develop certain conditions where if there is no abuse or name calling or slurs and slanders then things just don't feel normal. Some develop and then become a person who crave a certain amount of negativity in their life just to feel okay.

I am not exactly one of these types of people, though I can openly admit I have had my moments.

So, what happens inside of us and what is our mind doing to us or what is it that we accept and allow? Here is an example, if you have ever noticed or can relate to the example, it does not mean I am talking about you these are just simple things that happen for many of us.

So, we have done the getting ready for the night out with friends and we have paused in front of the mirror just as we were leaving the house, we confirmed to ourselves with a little wink of an eye that we are looking great and off out we go. We arrive to meet our friends and one says "wow you look amazing" we know this as that is what we said to ourselves right before we left our home. For some bizarre reason, we are not convinced by our friends' compliment and we can now let our mind take over. Some things we might allow our mind say and depending where we can apply the brakes to our mind it could even get "crazy" once we begin to focus our mind on their comments.

What did they mean? "I look amazing"

Are they trying to be smart with me? Just because I don't have a rich husband or a great job to buy all the expensive clothes they do?

What do they think I should always look a shambles? That is how they see me "normally"?

Maybe I should have used less cologne or a little less hair gel, were they being smart with me?

Maybe my make-up is too much and they were trying to let me know in a nice way by overcompensating the compliment?

Somewhere amidst all these fast-acting thoughts that we are allowing our mind to run away with, our stomach may begin to feel just a little ache. We are viewing the room of all of our friends and we are slyly checking out how everybody looks and somewhere in our mind we are looking to compare ourselves to others. All this from a simple compliment and our mind has taken over. Is this just a lack of our own confidence and we do not know how to receive a compliment and just own it?

We can use the same example of "You look amazing" we say thank you and this reassurance confirms exactly how we felt about ourselves leaving the house that evening and we can also allow our mind to absorb the compliment and begin to feel amazing too. We have become so accustomed to the negatives that allowing our mind run away with some thoughts almost seems like an easier process for us. When we take a look at it though, we can see how in order to have our mind and our feelings all in sync with each other, the simpler route is being okay with the compliment and any mind racing just does not occur. This is a win result for how we might begin on creating a new life for ourselves where we do not allow our mind race off on us and we can take a compliment, which goes against the grain of how society has been preparing us and we can actually feel good about ourselves.

I choose feeling good as often as I can and so I take compliments.

You can too.

We all can actually. We can all begin understanding that it is not what the person had to say to us that brings about any affect in our life. It is how we absorb it. How we may have been conditioned to accept people's words and again our own viewpoint. We find it hard to see another person's viewpoint. It may be possible in the example I am using to see it from the reverse. The person who said to you "you look amazing", let's imagine what their mind might be saying to them.

They always look nicer than me.

How come even though they earn less and wear cheaper clothes they manage to outshine everybody and always look so good?

I wish I could just show up looking fabulous as easily as they do.

No, we do not need to be so analytical of every little compliment we receive in life, of course not. This is just an example. What it can help us do though is to understand that we might have been so caught up by our own mind taking us over that we did not or could not even imagine the person paying to us the compliment maybe they simply have just a better view of us than we have of ourselves. Or they might just not have a great view of themselves. Either way it is an interesting concept to begin to see how our mind can set off racing at even the simplest thing and can bring about for us some feelings. It is through our feelings and our thoughts that we can live well and enjoy life, or we can live unwell and find life difficult. All by how we understand and interpret our own point of view and have an open enough mind to understand that there are other points of view which may differ from our own.

This can help us to see how, we are not all the same and we do not think the same and we do not feel the same. Some can just take the compliment and feel amazing for it. Think of how you have heard words like "I never gave it a second thought". This can be something we can practice and make attempts in our life to use on a daily basis. Not even a second thought or we could say to ourselves that we will not think negatively about anything for a single second.

This kind of practice is not always easy and sounds much easier than it can be. Some simple steps I like to use to clear my mind and allow myself to be blank for just a moment is my breathing. I could call it a form of mediation. Concentrating on my breathing, allowing myself to hear my lungs take in the air, feeling my nostrils as they fill and how they change shape as I exhale.

We can try it now; it is a simple exercise and can take us two minutes only. Get yourself seated comfortably. Ass in the chair and back somewhat straight, no slouching lol. Feet steadily on the floor and flat. We can say, feet can be placed at shoulders width apart and place your hands, palm down on your knees. It is a good idea to close your eyes but if you are somewhere that you do not want to close your eyes, well, it is not essential, but it helps.

*Take a large deep breath in and hold it for a second or two.

*Exhale slowly and steadily.

*Inhale another deep breath and hold for a second or two and breathe out gently but steadily again.

*Bring your mind to focus on how your nose is working to deliver you this wonderful air. Feel the breath as it fills your lungs. The process occurring is, air is transferring through your lungs and delivering oxygen to your red blood cells.

*Continue the deep breathing.

Feel how the air coming in is not only in your lungs, feel the oxygen moving through your body in your blood cells. Feel the goodness flow through your body.

*Breathe in through your nose and feel the way in which your nose opens to take in the new air.

*Breathe out through your mouth, feel how your mouth muscles will form to breathe out the unwanted air and feel the nastiness flow out.

*Breathing in again and feel how your feet are touching the ground. This is so significant of how the term being grounded and having your feet firmly on the floor. Feel how your posture is benefiting from the air you are breathing in.

As you exhale feel the unwanted parts and pieces of negative energies flow out from your body.

With each new breath in, you are delivering to your body exactly the oxygen that is needed to live, to survive and to exist. These oxygen particles are flowing calmly through your body bringing new energy and a nice calm feeling to all of your muscles.

Allow your muscles to be relaxed, only thinking of how your nose and mouth are operating to breathe in and breathe out. With each breath in comes new life, new attitude, new thoughts. With each exhale leaves the negative energy you have been holding on to. Breathing out is preparing you for more good air on the next inhale.
Having your eyes closed can help you envision the path in which the oxygen is taking in your body. Your mind can begin to slow down and all of your feelings of touch and smell and taste can come together to embrace the new life you are bringing to your mind. It is not unusual to begin to feel

emotional at this point in the exercise and itis okay to let the emotions out with each breath you exhale. As you exhale the emotional parts of you, you may begin to feel stronger every time you inhale. As it is this new air that is preparing you for your day or for the rest of your day.

We had discussed earlier that our minds may very well be a coming together of our senses and our emotions and how your brain feels inside. Allow the breathing to work its way all the way to your head. As you breath in, the head is becoming clearer for you. The body is becoming relaxed and your emotions are feeling calm and refreshed. Through this breathing exercise you can begin to calm your mind to a place where you can slowly open your eyes and allow the day back into your life. Slowly opening your eyes and taking notice of the items around you. Seeing life as if it were your first time all over again.

It is with a calm mind and a cleared-out mind that our emotional self can feel and become excited about our day. We can feel energy towards our day, we can feel a smile beginning across our face. Raise up from your seated position and walk a little. Maybe outside in nature where you can hear the world around you. This world is where you belong and your being part of it is very much a valuable piece of the entire bigger picture.

It is through our breathing exercise that our mind can find the tiny break it needs to recover from all of the over thinking we have developed habits of doing. It is our mind connected with our emotion and our senses that can now tackle any task in our day.

Should you find any day escaping you or anytime your mind begins to race, this breathing exercise can help you to become grounded and clear. This can be like having a little reset button all to ourselves right slap, bang in our day at any time when we feel we need it.

Our choice is to allow our mind to be over worked. We also possess the ability to stop ourselves in a frantic state of mind and choose to do some breathing. We can choose to allow a peace and calm come over all of our senses and bring into our day a clear and calm mind which will help us focus. This focus is invaluable to our well-being and can help us take on any challenge, get through any day and deal with life and all of the people in it.

I hope you will try the breathing as often as you need and remember to mix it up a little by trying it outside in nature, in the park. Sometimes it might be just as you are about to head into a sales meeting or while waiting to pick up the kids from school and you are just stealing a moment for yourself while sitting in park in the car. This little rest in your day will help you to enjoy everything that comes next. If you need to practice your breathing more often in the beginning, that is okay too. As you practice this technique more and more over time, your body will learn it as a habit, it will become an easier exercise for you and more fulfilling the more you practice.

It is a beautiful thing to feel alive and have a mind that is clear. It is a beautiful way to be that no matter who may say what to you that it has no power over your well-being and your thoughts are clear. Being happy to be alive is a wonderful feeling that I wish I could just package up and gift to everybody. Allowing our mind those moments to relax and focus, brings to us not only a clear head but also a very deep emotional feeling too. These feelings will slow down through time and allowing them out is a great way to become calmer in all of our daily tasks or chores. Realizing that there is no need for any rapid thinking and no need to outthink any other human or situation in our life. Our life is about us breathing. The importance of our breath is the simplest and single basic thing that we must have to survive. And only for a few minutes each day.

This exercise can bring immense benefits and can show us exactly how, that with our mind clear and calm we can live so full and joyful. We can begin again on any given day. This allows us to see how we do actually have a choice. It is our choice if we are willing to breathe to allow ourselves some small moments of clear mind into our life.

I guess a simple important factor to take note would be in how we always have a choice. We can choose to allow our mind to become loaded with negatives. We can choose to feel our way, way down by following such thoughts. By contrast, we can choose to relax our mind. We can choose to allow our feelings flow and begin to enjoy life with a calm and peaceful mind.

YOU DECIDE!

Practical discussion with SELF.

Being human is a weird and wonderful thing, isn't it though? We cannot figure anything out of a simple nature, yet some go around figuring out how to beat the stock market trends and make loads of money and live very comfortably from it. There are others who work, day in and day out doing research of either a chemical nature or a scientific nature. These kinds of people can basically all tell the future, so to speak.

Through studying trends and patterns and mutations in life, they are able to figure stuff out. Geniuses I suppose we could call them. The question I pose is that and it is a belief of mine though not everybody can be tarred with the same brush. My belief is that even the millionaires who have such success in Wall street have issues they need help with regularly. The rocket scientist and the "BioChem" genius just like me and you have little quirky ways about them that maybe they too wish to change or correct in their personal life. There are those who today will venture into their workplace and mastermind how to make a microchip even smaller and figure out how it can go into the next new light weight phone and make a bundle from their work. Do they get sweaty palms when they are asked to discuss their breakthrough inventions? There is a good chance they do. Does anxiety have a boundary it doesn't cross inside of humans mapped out by their success levels? No, this would be the easy answer to this kind of question. People are people first, who they are by way of their career is not what defines any person. The bank balance held by any one individual is not an access card to total serenity nor a membership to any great club that claims to make life wonderful always. It just does not happen that disorders or social awkwardness holds back and only graces those of us who work a so-called normal 9 to 5 or even less.

Emotional health is not something only available to the rich and famous. Nope, such emotional health is available to us all. A clear mind as we were just talking about is not reserved only for those who wish to fly and clone life so as to exist on planet Mars. Nope, humans are humans just like you and me, we all are different by way of the simple things, like how we all have different fingerprints. Many of us have different hair colour or eye colour and we come in all kinds of shapes and sizes. What we do have in common is the way in which we can feel very similar things, not always at the same time but we can gain understandings of how we felt and what we thought and by sharing them with others we can learn how similar in these areas we are and just to say again, bank balances and intellectual abilities have not got much to do with these feelings or emotional well-being.

What does be practical with us actual mean to any of us?

Practicality can seem like it is a foreign language to many. We may not like to be too practical in our life as it feels just a little "square" or "boring". A good friend used to make me laugh when he would say, "oh screw that, I am more of a flamboyant type guy", he was not gay or anything, what he meant was he just used to like to be able to be free in himself, free spirited I guess and too much practicality made him feel rigid or hemmed in a little bit.

Are there areas in your own life that you feel hemmed in? Do you ever feel like there is a huge piece of you that wished you had rebelled against all kinds of regime and rules? There is nothing wrong with these ideas and or if you have indeed rebelled. The practicality can often show us how some things are a good idea and how other ideas about life are not such good ideas.

I am fully aware that here in my writing these words that you are reading them. My voice in your head right now is the voice you have conjured up to imagine how I am talking and more than likely your own voice is telling you the words at times too. This would be the beauty of our being able to have imagination and allow our thoughts create what my voice might sound like right now. The practical side of it is that I am typing and you are reading. That is pretty straight forward and simple, isn't it?

The discussion to have with ourselves comes in many different angles or points of view. Something practical to us might be off the wall to another person. This is exactly where having a discussion with SELF may just be a great way to help reduce stress and anxiety levels within our own world.

What can a practical discussion with self even mean?

There are times that we will review how we think about ourselves. While taking a look at ourselves from the outside we will begin by liking ourselves very much. This is not the quick glance in the mirror I was mentioning earlier. This is something a little deeper where we actually begin to imagine ourselves to be someone different. We do this by comparison. It is by our friends and peers that we have created inside our own heads a scale upon which we form judgement. We are marvelous creatures for making things inside of our heads that allow us to bring ourselves down. We begin to compare; how do we rate in our social circles. No, you are not on your own on this one, everyone does it. It all started back when we were little babies and then we met another little toddler and we noticed that they cry a lot. We did not know that we were forming opinions inside our tiny little minds all the way back then, but we were.

Imagine a little toddler and he is on one of his early days of visiting the playground. There is another little toddler there too and they have not been out in the world much either. For toddlers, their first years are often being held on the hip of their mom and have learned about the world from an adult point or angle of view. A toddler has become used to seeing other children but mostly has had their interaction with other adults up to a certain age. Maybe 2 or 3 for example. This first day in the playground and being at their own height and eye level they come face to face with another little person just like themselves. The new life, out ready for exploration in life sees another child and notices things about them. Not so much in how they look but more about the way in which they act. The parents are standing close by and chatting and all life seems wonderful, "oh he is very mature for his age" one parent is saying to the other and the replies go back and forth "well I find at night he is...." and so on. The toddler knows absolutely nothing about psychology or studying behavioral patterns but that is what the baby is doing. They watch the other little person as they are right around their own eye level, so it is strange and new, the inquisitiveness of toddlers is great to watch and see how they develop. If the newfound friend picks up some pebbles and throws them the other child will probably do it too. When one of the parents decides it is time to go and picks up their child, the other sees how the child begins a little tantrum. They might try this with their own parent immediately and here we have an indication of how the sponge of learning inside of us all was watching and learning from a very tiny age indeed. A child will watch the other children and see how they act and then try it with their own parents. We can tell from these behaviors that at a very young age we developed a system of copying what we see around us. We have become involved with comparing how we look and how we act from a very young age indeed.

There are a ton of clichés to mention all of the time about how an issue or item of life can be easily explained. The best here I feel would be "we learn what we live with" which basically suggests much of our behavior is just like how we started out that day in the playground, we watch and we copy and we learn. Sometimes any such behavior we try out may not work for us and we just drop it and move on to the next. We copy others too; a little boy wants to mimic his dad by the way he will try and soap his face to shave. A little girl will play with her hair or brush her dolls hair just the way mammy brushes hers. These are all little things we have picked up on somewhere along our journey, we never gave much thought to them because they are what we can consider just a normal part of growing and developing.

As grown adults now though, it is not trial and error anymore. We are not afforded such a wide berth in developing our behaviors and we might be cut off from our social groups if we start just acting out and childish, so we find ways to hide little ways about ourselves on the inside. There are some traits we will allow out to our close friends and there are others we save for only when we are alone and able to speak directly to ourselves with nobody else around.

When we talk to ourselves and begin to see ourselves, it is not always in the best light. No, not that we keep the lights off, the way in which we have been comparing to others, the way in which we see things about ourselves that we do not like and we see things in others that we believe we really like. You see, we carry a little critic around with us in our life too. It goes back to some of the thing's society has some responsibility for. The little things that have been allowed to develop within the society we have grown accustomed to. The idea of how it is all perfectly normal to criticize and none better to do such to us than ourselves. The normalization of how it is okay to be critical. We have been hearing criticism all around us from a very young age and it has taken a grip inside of ourselves. We may never completely silence the critic; we can however take a good shot at keeping it very silent for long periods of time. We will get to the critic a little later on though.

It is the comparing to others that is slowly but surely wearing away at us like the way in which a river will wear away a rock and eventually make the river create a new course. Water is soft and simple, a liquid that can be shattered by our own hand, yet the large rock of stone cannot be budged by us. It is too hard and too heavy, another saying "even a dripping faucet can wear away a stone" imagine just drip drip, one drip at a time, powerful enough to crumble the hard rock. How amazing is that?

We, the humans have our own little drip going on inside of ourselves and it is in the form of the critic coupled with the way in which we like to compare ourselves to others.

We try out a few different trends and styles of how we carry ourselves through our teenage years and just as we did when we were toddlers, we are trying what we see around us and we will settle for what works for that time. This would suggest all totally normal right? Again, society has made acceptable the normalization of trends and fashions, how we can look or how we might even think.

Couples can clash a little in a relationship and the conversation can be how "why can't we just be like them, look over there, those two-walking hand in hand". Comparing our life to someone else's. The clothes we wear or the haircut we might get, all part of how other people are. These are fine because they are on the outside and can be changed easily. We can make drastic changes to our appearances in a matter of moments, for me a haircut and a shave and choose some different clothing, I could creep up on people who would swear they knew me. I could walk right up to them actually and they would not recognize me, just by a change of appearance on the outside.

The changes however on the inside are not as easy to make. The behavior we have been comparing ourselves to has become such habit and now part of us that we can run in to difficulties and not as easily wiped away as easy as a quick shave. Or are they? Just like back when we were a toddler and meeting that other little baby, we have been developing our inner self too. We have been molding and changing ever so slightly all the way along. We may now find ourselves confronting ourselves and thinking we are not as happy as others. We are not as wealthy as others and we do not have such true love others have. If you have ever found yourself having these kinds of conversations with yourself, then you have probably tip toed along the borders of depression or a feeling of being down inside of yourself. There is a good chance that you have gotten anxious over silly stuff too and found some social gatherings a little awkward. Why? Because these things all didn't just happen overnight and who we have become as people has been a long time in the making.

Imagine for a moment. The person you are right now is a person that has been developing for years. WOW!

This totally makes sense and all the times you have tried to make little changes have been so difficult because it is who you are. The person you are has been the same person all the way along since the years of being way younger. The beauty of this is that there is nothing wrong with you, in fact even typing the word is something I do not like. The idea that there is anything wrong with anybody is totally WRONG.

We all just develop a little differently from each other. Some faster and then of course some slower. We comprehend at different rates and just like our angles from where we see stuff, we all see a little differently. This can be a little satisfying to know and yes, I am about to say it. There is nothing wrong with you.

How we try and compare ourselves to others is probably the single most thing we must stop doing immediately. Cut it out. You are you; you are the person you have always been and it is time to let the world know who you are. When you feel any particular way or another, let it out. Be you.

This may seem like an awful difficult thing to do as when we have developed habits to compare ourselves to others and we have developed strategies to hide our true self from the world around us, I mean it is a strategy that has been developing from back when we were two years of age even. How can we just change that now?

We begin by having some practical discussion with ourselves. What might we begin to discuss? Let's try a few simple questions and answers.

Am I a movie star with all the money in the world? No.

Am I a fashion model who enjoys all around the world photography shoots? No.

Am I a professional athlete who wears my country's flag at international competitions? No.

Am I a talented musician who travels the world playing concerts? No.

Am I a skilled engineer who earns large paychecks for doing skilled work of any kind? No.

Am I a celebrity of any kind? No.

Am I a gifted craftsman that makes beautiful structures or artwork for all to adore and admire? No. Am I talented in anyway where the public can recognize me?

No. Am I the go to person in my group of friends for advice and friendly encouragement? No.

Am I anybody? Yes, yes you are. This is great that through a simple process of elimination we can come to the good part. All the other things can take a long jump into a river. By being practical with ourselves we can determine exactly who we are, what we are, we can dig even deeper too.

Do I have skills of my own? Yes.

Am I a loving person? Yes.

Do I have compassion? Yes.

Do people actually like my company? Yes.

Do I have something to offer the world? Yes.

Am I able to help my fellow humans? Yes.

Do I have the ability to be kind? Yes.

Do I have the ability to make a difference in my community? Yes.

Am I able to not compare my life to anybody else's anymore? Yes.

Are we beginning to see that when we begin to get practical and well, let's just call it "more simple" or "more basic", it is then that we can begin to see some SELF worth? We cannot just overnight become oozing with confidence and not the fake confidence either that many people have to wear a brave face for to carry it off on a daily basis. We can ask ourselves some practical questions and begin to see that we are actually somebody. We can help others and begin to feel alive and contributing in our society. We can go freely into our workplace and be quite comfortable with all who we meet and have no problems delivering any work items to our colleagues without sweaty palms or nerves or anxieties. Why can we do these things so easily?

When we recognize who we are inside, we are the same person we have always known ourselves to be. When we slow down our mind and we figure out how to acknowledge to ourselves that we are special and we mean a lot in our world. Then, yes then we can walk tall and mean it. We can begin to glow in our circles, we will not be doing anything different, how and ever the people around us can sense it when you are "on". People will begin to slowly make comments like, "I don't know what you are doing or who you have become but it is beautiful" some will even get jealous and try and peg you back down with some criticisms. It is these people that can be your recharging of your batteries and keep you going from strength to strength. No more second guessing who or what was I and what does it mean to you. No. It is the comments and the haters for want of a better term to describe those who will not like you to just be you. Then you will begin to recognize even more of how it has been your circle of friends who were well suited by your own shyness. It suited them to have you around, you fit into their idea of who you are and who you should be. Funny thing is they only knew the you that you allowed them to see. Your own critics kept you hiding for too long. These are some very powerful results of having some conversations with yourself on a grounded and practical level.

We do not have to walk so tall as to shadow anyone who is still stuck inside themselves and spending their time comparing their life with anyone else's. No, we can walk just tall enough to allow our brightness shine on them and there will never be a shadow. How is it that we can make these transformations? I hear you asking. We begin by allowing our self a little time to have a chat with ourselves. We bring about a focus of who we are. We put an end to consuming ourselves with who others are and how we compare to them. We put an end to playing the role that everybody else sees best fits us. We slowly and steadily just as we have begun to practice how we can use breathing to allow our mind to focus. We slowly start to allow the same person, the exact same person we have always been to come out and say hello to the world. We begin to introduce the real you to the people around you. No more brave face, no more saying I am okay when I am not okay. Simple steps, slow baby steps even. Remember we have been this person since we were very young and baby like, so baby steps would be a very good way to proceed. It is by having a practical discussion with ourselves about who we are that we can begin to turn over stones that we thought may have just gone and left us. The who we are that we thought was gone because we advanced from teenager into adulthood.

There is no shame at all in catching yourself in front of the mirror and staring at ourselves and you know what? Let's do it now as a little exercise. Stand in front of a mirror. Try and be by yourself to save you from hiding inside, look directly at yourself in the eye and say these words.

"I love you; I am so glad that we are finally going to begin being who I am. I love you for taking this step towards happiness and our future. You are a valuable member of this planet and this planet is there for you.

I love you".

The Partner

In our life we have the need or feel the need to have friends and then quite often we have a select few that we refer to as best friends. There are those of us who may have found a true lover and we call them our partner. We feel like they are the one human being that understands us so well that we can even call them our soul mate. The one living human being on the planet that, we enjoy their company, we love how they look, we feel good inside when they are around us in any way.

They can leave us a note and when we read it, we get all warm inside. We see how they act out of love and we just get emotional by their compassion that we feel, wonderful really. All of the good they do in our life; we really feel what they mean to us and so we love them. For this we call them partner. There is something about how they are around us and we can allow our guard down and really show them our true self and they do not judge us. They are the person who when we are at our most vulnerable, they offer us that very important shoulder to lay our head. Even their embrace, a hug can mean so much to us and there are even possibilities that we have sought refuge in this person many times in our life. This is our partner....

Now we can or I can continue writing this fairy tale idea of who our partner is and though it is quite ideal and romantic, if you have this such person in your life, you are not only loved but very lucky. Remembering that we are all growing up within the same society that has cleverly shown us what is acceptable and what is normal. Well our partner has also grown up within the same limitations and it may be difficult for them to really understand who we are. There are times that we misunderstand each other as partners and we pull and tug at opposite ends in different directions.

In order to understand our partner and what it is we absolutely adore about them; it would be fair to say we must have a very good understanding of ourselves. We know or are beginning to understand that based upon what we learned as we have grown, perhaps our partner learned similar morals and carries similar opinions. These may well have been what caused an attraction in the beginning. These things could have been the vibes we sensed about our partner and helped us to fall in love with them.

Fall in love with them, isn't that a nice little thought though. Thinking about how we fell in love.

Should we decide or make decisions to transform our own lives and begin to practice gentle meditation and speak to ourselves in the mirror and start some fresh techniques to love ourselves, how on earth is our partner going to understand this? Can we grow and possibly outgrow our partner? It is possible that we may wish to be loving and the same person they fell in love with might begin changing. We are not changing drastically or anything like that. We are just becoming who we have always been and there is a possibility that our partner may not like who we really are deep down inside.

Like, yeah for sure we can make changes to ourselves and have no problem recognizing that work colleagues are not enough of a factor in our lives that we need not worry about their opinion of us enough that we might fear making changes to our own body and mind. We do not have enough of a bond with other parents in our community, so that will not be a problem for us to make changes. We do not have to hide our personal self from any of these people outside in the world. We might tread along with some cautions and merely knowing who we are inside will be enough to keep us from slipping back into an overly self-conscious state that we become in a mind-bending experience and start to shake and lose it all. No not at all, we have our breathing to practice and are free to take time out on any given day. We can handle all those outside folks. Though, what about our partner? Change in our lives can be emotional and change can be painful. Just like I had mentioned before the breathing techniques. When you practice often you will probably find in the beginning that emotions seem to come out of nowhere. To a partner looking on, they might not understand what exactly is going on. Why did we just go upstairs to be by ourselves and why now can they hear us crying or weeping to ourselves. Having a partner in our life and making some little changes, allowing our guard down and becoming who we have always been can bring about some unusual times between us and our partner.

As we spend some time rediscovering who we are and all the beautiful feelings we begin enjoying, it will be nice to share as much of them as we can with our partner. It could be possible that a partner of ours could try to throw this book out in the bin as they do not like what they are witnessing. They might say "ever since you started reading that book you have gone and turned into a mad person" lol. This would be just the normal run of things; remember they belong to the same society we have been dodging bullets in for years. Criticisms are all part of a way of "normal" life now. We all use them, it is not a lacking piece of anybody's character, those who choose not to be too critical, well yes, they are the ones you should stick to like glue.

Having a partner is a great thing and you will probably begin to infect your partner with some slight undertones of beauty while you work on yourself. The sixth sense of us humans begins to sniff it out and when we are changing from a closed up old box with sharp corners to a more grounded individual with beauty and calmness, a partner will notice and be confused and wondering why? It is possible to infect our partner with self-growth and this is a great way for two people to start over. There does not have to be any reason to start over, there does not have to have been any issues. Starting over together can be as wonderful as the first times you shared together. This can bring about romance just like never before.

It is wonderful and is to be enjoyed. There are many of us who are single and we are searching for a partner. Let us consider the single role and see how some of our dating profiles or chat up lines might read

Single, slightly neurotic, have had occasion to be, nervous breakdown ready but have a killer smile. (no dates from that)

Single, approx. 10 years, just never found the right person. (too picky, no dates there)

How about some new ones though?

Single a while, have been working on myself and rediscovering who I am and I am in love. I wish to share this newfound beauty with a partner (they are falling at your feet already), too good to be true.

Single, used to spend way too much time freaking out about the tiniest of things. Am way over that now and looking for someone to really enjoy life with. (yup a true soul mate can be found)

Tiny differences can make a whole bunch of sense to another single person who is searching for the exact things that you are. The critics will say automatically "too good to be true". Those who are genuine will recognize the beauty that you are beginning to live in to.

We are all searching for that one true friend, lover or partner. They do exist and they are out there. If you are single and you have lost interest in searching for someone. Apply breathing techniques to your search. When you are calm and have kind of stopped looking, they are more than likely to just show up. Unexpected and ready to fall in love. We all deserve a partner and sometimes they are taken from us too soon in life and we can spend years pining for them.

Some of us will remain single forever and this is totally acceptable and fine too. It is not that we must have someone to lean on. It is when we begin to love ourselves inside and out that we begin to learn that a partner is not a necessity. We want a person in our life, yes this is good. It is by no way a necessity at all. When we are loving ourselves, we can find less and less time for other people to be that close to us.

Having a partner might just slow down our own process of self-discovery and we are best to walk this path by ourselves. It is going to be important that we do not make excuses to ourselves for not working on self because of a partner or a love that we have for another person. The path to loving ourselves is a selfish type of path anyway and we could do without too many criticisms no matter how innocent they seem. It is never another person's fault, or it is never that another person is the reason we feel something. Yes, a partner can be the stimulus to bring about feelings inside of ourselves. A funny thing I have heard people say many times "you make me feel...." or "I hate the way they make me feel". These ideas that it is another person that is choosing what feeling we decide to dwell on, well to be honest, is ridiculous.

Our feelings come and go and if you remember earlier, we were talking about this exact thing. Feelings come and go and what we decide to do about them is very much within our own power. It is upon me if I wish to choose to allow myself to become down and disgusted about anything. It is my choice to sit around and wallow in my feelings. I choose and I decide, these are the powers we have over ourselves. Remember our own mind and how it is within our entire being that these feelings are occurring.

Whether single or attached, searching or not searching, the answers to ourselves are all from within, inside of us. A partner can be a great rock to lean on but is not a necessity. It is our decision to allow our self out to the world that will give great benefit to any partner we may have around us or to any new partner that may come along. This is a journey of self, is about self and the questions all come from self. The answers come from self too. It is not validation from another human being that will bring about within us a feeling of any greater being. It is the validation inside of our own body, mind and spirit that will bring about the great benefit to all who are around us.

A life journey to SELF is possible within a relationship and outside of one. All who will benefit will benefit. Those who do not wish to, will not. Imagine, it is really that simple.

These are part and parcel some of the beauties of life itself. Everything is simple. We were once babies who understood things in a very basic way. Our own innocence kept us happy and playful. The basic goodness of life we believed in, it was all so magical when we were, "once upon a time" little. Life and being an adult have caused quite a bit of confusion since then. It us adults who confuse it all. Society has allowed us to develop this way, so we are not entirely to blame as we have had a strong nudge every so often by society around us.

When and if we wish to simplify everything, we can. How? Just break it down to basic understanding that makes sense to you. Think like a 3-year-old might think.

Simple and basic, may just be the key to your new partner. A life of bliss.

Life on its Terms

There are oh so many ways in which we can find ourselves just a little bit guilty of wanting it all and wanting things exactly how we want them too. We look to the glam and glitz of Hollywood and we see a superficial lifestyle that we believe is real and the exact way in which we believe we were destined to live. It just does not work out that way for the majority of us. There are however many philosophies that suggest if we want something bad enough all we have to do is set our mind to it and we can achieve it. Perhaps then there is indeed an easy fix to getting what we want. Just go out and take it would be how some might encourage you. I really do love this idea as I also believe in the concept. So how do we make a concept become reality?

Hard work towards any of our goals can be just another cliché or it can also be a definite strategy to achieve results. We have all been encouraged somewhere along our path to keep our head down and focus on our dreams, that our dreams can come true if we work hard to get to them. Here is where we might have found where the almighty critic inside of us could raise their ugly head and make attempts at convincing us that in actual reality, we have no chance and we are deluding ourselves into a false sense of nonsense. Let us repeat right about here, that if we choose to listen to our inner critic it is not the critic that is winning, oh no. It is the person inside of ourselves, yup me and you again that is making a conscious choice to not allow ourselves to continue on our path of dream chasing. So, we give up.

I say that I believe in the concept as I believe there are more parts to the equation or more pieces to the puzzle that we must figure out first. Pieces and puzzle already sound puzzling, doesn't it?

If we focus our mind, we can make a great number of breakthroughs in our life. We can achieve anything we want if we set our mind to it. This will require us to remain totally focused and devoted to our goal. Doesn't sound too hard either, so why do so many of us kind of fall short a little bit? I can hear you even speaking the words before I get to them, because it can be too darn hard, that's why. Could we say that is a very defeatist type attitude? Of course, we can say that, as a matter of fact we can refer to it any way in which we choose to. There are no right and wrong ways to achieve anything. Some proven methods though are that, should we stay focused and continue with dedication then yes, we can achieve and achieve beyond what we ever even first believed. Let's take a look at some reality checks though first. It is important that I play devil's advocate from time to time to keep us grounded.

I would safely say that a person born and in receipt of such genetic make-up that they will never grow taller than 5 feet tall, let's say. I cannot imagine that they will be the NBA all-star slam dunk contest winner too many years in a row. I would also say they might never even try out for basketball as this is a sport that is heavily dominated by much taller persons. Although there was a very short slam dunk contest winner in previous years.

I could also say that for example a person is blind from birth, I cannot believe that they will hold a position of highest ranked officer in the military sniper rifle ranks.

There would also be the person who has a genetic inheritance of baldness that might never break the Guinness book of records attempt at having the longest hair in the world.

The examples I am using are highlighting how by way of genetic make-up on how we formed in the womb there may very well be some restrictions upon us from the very first moment we enter the world. There we go again a reference back to when we were a baby, many things were already set in place for us. The examples I have mentioned also make for a little sprinkle of reality that some things may never occur and so because of our genes that we inherit we may not be able to or possess the ability to achieve everything we set our minds on. And this is where we can bring to an end the idea of restrictions and limitations. The concept that I agree on is we do indeed possess the ability to achieve a ton more than we might ever have even imagined. How?

The examples I am using are due to inherited genes as we formed as a person, outside of genes what else might stop us from achieving our goals? Nothing really, that is right, nothing. We can set goals and the more extreme the goal perhaps the more extreme the training or workload to achieve it may have to be. We have within ourselves an ability to shut out all kinds of negatives and we can block out people from our lives that do not believe in the dream that we believe in. A difficult piece is undoing the embedded nature within ourselves, of how society has conditioned us to believe in less and less of our own abilities.

Not every single person born can be president of a country for example. The reason for this would be the term in which a president sits in office and so with the passing of 4 or more years each presidential term, well the birthing rate happens a little faster and so not every person will ever get their chance even if it were to just be offered on a rotation type basis. There are limitations set upon us in life by time and how much of it we actually have and how often our turn may come around. What it does not mean is that it is not possible for anyone to become president of their country. This is very possible and can begin at the ripe young age of toddler. There are many things we can condition ourselves, to actually do. We do not have to be as extreme as wanting to be president of our county. We do not even have to be as extreme as winning

Olympic medals or selling out a blockbuster Hollywood movie hit. What we can do is find an achievable goal that appears more realistic to our own genetic make-up and within our time span of life. Achievable goals are meant to be achieved I hear you say, that is why they are called achievable.

A goal in life can be to become stress free. Lose our overanxious mind set. We can set our mind to become the highest rank in our own job. We can aim for top sales position of the year, employee of the month, world's greatest parent. We can strive to use our brain power for academic studies and become a rocket scientist if we should so choose to do so. These are achievable, though they sound extreme, they are totally doable for everyone should they again, choose.

The concept is, to put our mind to achieving something and we can do it.

There will always be distractions and other people who might step into our way and cause a diversion so to speak. We may have our heart set on becoming the highest achieving student in our college. A few peers get in the way and invite us or shame us into a few party's through the college year and we may find ourselves distracted and not make the desired target. We may wish to undertake something a little simpler in our lifetime, perhaps we have a desire to be an absolute great golfer. We will require a ton of practice and a lot of dedication to the golf club to be out there practicing in any of the weather that may come our way. We will have to put in the effort to continue dedicated and go for our dream.

Let's add in some children and a nice little family home, here we will find more distractions. We need to pick children up from school, we have to pay our mortgage and so we must spend time at work in our job. The children need caring for and so we cannot devote the time we need to all day fairway walking sessions. It just isn't practical.

It would then come about that how about if we are to start out even a little lower with where we set our sights. Can we say that in actual reality we can become a better person? Can we consider what may be an achievable goal could be to get in touch with our inner self and begin to live free from any fears or elements that we may have thought have been holding us back in our life? Can we learn about ourselves and what is our role within our family dynamic, can we learn how to not offend our fellow humans here on our planet and is it possible that with a right frame of mind perhaps we can achieve anything.

We are of course leaving aside that there are certain types of hard work that we must put in to reach our goals. This work can be swamped with distractions of all kinds and from every angle imaginable too. This would bring me back to suggesting achievable goals where we can use the tools that we have inside of ourselves naturally. A terrific artist may never set foot inside of a gallery with the full intentions of having a show or an exhibition being the farthest thing from their mind. They will continue their art though; they will not focus on other aspects of possible failure or success.

The journey of their art is the art itself.

Others may gain appreciation of their work and bring it to public eyes and so the artist may then be recognized as one of the all-time greats and admired for their work. The artist already knew this about their work every day they set foot inside of the door into their studio. The greatness and the recognition are something that came from society, from the world outside of the artist's mind. It is the outside factors that have set the standard of greatness, yet how did the artist create such great art? Their own standard of greatness came from within. The hard work was put in inside of their own studio, quite possibly all by themselves.

Today in life many of us may have visited a gallery or two and paused in front of pictures or paintings of some of the greatest artists through the ages of history. We pause and admire their work and see beauty in their paintings. We believe in how great they actually are and were. What we might not consider is the life or the actual person behind the great art. We might not give thought about how perhaps they were depressed or eccentric. We can learn of the stories and history surrounding these great artists and learn how they pined for a life they could not have, they wallowed in self-pity. In their own era the society surrounding them had a different set of standards and many artists were considered "MAD" the society of their time made things quite difficult for them as they were not seen to be the great achievers in the colleges and were not the absolute top of the intellect ladder. I am not referring to any artists in particular, only to highlight to you that as society has changed their standards, only then did the full recognition of their greatness become apparent. The artist of their era however did not stop creating their work. They did not give up. It is quite possible that it was very hard for them out in the public world or in public life as their own true expression was jeered and mocked. To consider how hard it might have been for them to be somewhat of an outcast of their society shows how believing in themselves and not allowing the rules or standards of society dictate to themselves. They continued their work and they believed in themselves. They did not listen to those who jeered them, they always pressed on with their passion regardless.

Can we express ourselves just as a great artist can? Is it possible that we can work hard in the studio of ourselves while never bowing down to the standard society has set outside of ourselves?

Yes, we can, we can achieve many great things that society will recognize us for. The fact that life is going on all around us and people are hating on each other and being overly critical and even telling each other how they should live or what they should believe in as far as faith. Are these societal limitations something we should concern ourselves with?

The true greatness of your own personal work on yourself may never be recognized until hundreds of years later. This is something to keep in mind when digging inside of our own personal self. Awakening our mind in its entirety, our emotions and our thoughts to look inside and develop our own great works of art by bringing into our life the beauty of who we actually are. Remembering the person, we were as a child. Just like the great artists who have created masterpiece works of art, we can be the canvas of where we make our own art. You yes, you are the masterpiece you can create. Just like how the artist never allowed the public to come into their studio and view their work is very similar to how you do not have to permit others to come and view your work or to criticize you, they will criticize anyway. It is your choice to accept their criticisms and allow such to affect you negatively. Look at the artists of our history, some were shunned and yet they still went back to the studio and kept working. They may have had a ton of feelings they wanted to let out by screaming from the roof tops, but they continued working. They expressed themselves in a way they found comfort in.

An interesting word or phrase "finding comfort", many of us would love to just find a peaceful moment or two between our ears, find some comfort in how the world might welcome us or receive us in our daily lives. I get this and understand it very well. And to be honest that is why this exact chapter has the title it has. We must accept life on the terms that it comes with. We can have a desire and a passion to change the society and the standards and the rules, of course this is a great fire to have inside of you. The terms that life comes with though, may be that the change you wish to see or perform is out of reach, it could be considered a goal that is not achievable. We can add to our stress and anxiety by wanting to make the changes and engage in battle with life and become more entangled in all kinds of emotions that can imprison us, should we choose to allow it. Again, the words "choice" and "allow" are mentioned here totally on purpose to just remind us that all the time the effects of things around us can be our choice to allow them in or not allow them in. These could be for example, other people's words, the standard set by society of what are acceptable levels of greatness. The criticisms people may offer to us without us ever asking for it and of course our own critic inside that continues to fool us with fake fears. Yes, fear is real, the fake aspect is how our own critic inside might play very hard to keep us down or stuck and hold us back from ever trying.

Life is harsh and life is cruel, please do not make any mistake that it is all a bed of roses and everybody and everything is wonderful. Life on its terms can be a very difficult time even for the most balanced of people. The beauty and the masterpiece you can become is having an understanding of how cruel life can be and for this very reason there is absolutely no point in being cruel on yourself.

Each and every morning that you step outside your door into the world, you are prepared to take on the big cruel game of life. Nasty and horrible lurking on every corner, seeping up through cracks in the pavement. It is everywhere. What best favour could you do for yourself? Accept the world and the people in it even if you feel they do not accept you. A key to accepting the world can be easily discovered by accepting yourself. Knowing that genetically we have restrictions or limitations, the sands of time can make it difficult for us to achieve some goals, what we can achieve though is to be our own masterpiece, the beauty of you has a very valuable place in the world.

The mighty artists who created master pieces, remember they were considered fools some of them by their society, they knew what they toiled over was beauty and they knew the fools were really the ones who could not see. This might be a good time for a little exercise now that we are beginning to get a handle on how we do not need validation from the world outside of ourselves. Let's go to a mirror, look inside the mirror at your own face. Just your face and then your eyes, repeat the words out loud, not like shouting just speaking them out.

I accept life and the world outside; I accept the beauty I have inside. I AM BEAUTIFUL, I do not need the world's approval, I am a work of art. I am my very own MASTERPIECE.

I will hazard a guess that this exercise felt a little awkward. I get that and it is like anything we do, a little practice and a few times more, the awkwardness will slowly ease away. Try it once a day and see how you get on for a while.

Livable or Loveable

When we were young, well some of us at least lol, we had to do some chores for our parents. Wash dishes or vacuum a room or bring out some of the garbage. Chores they were called and we did them, sometimes grudgingly and other times we were over enthusiastic maybe even making a mess, this could have been a strategy in trying to keep our parents from asking us to do such a chore again ha-ha. It has been good preparation though for doing things we do not like and sometimes learning that if we just do not complain we can actually enjoy them. There are times in our careers or jobs, a boss may give us a task to do that we hate and we have a choice to either do it happily or do it sourly. I am not saying we are going to enjoy everything we have to do but there are always options for what we do and more so how we do them. You will take note I have brought up the concept of choice again as that is what it really is. We can choose to enjoy everything we are asked to do, or we can choose to hate it. We always have a choice. From growing up and learning about chores I obtained a hard work type ethic that was very simple. Get stuck in and then it will be over soon and no big deal. Get on with it, no matter how I felt about something, when it is something I must do, the only way to be rid of the feeling of disgust or unhappy was to tackle the task at hand and get to the finish as efficiently and promptly as possible.

So, what is with the livable & the lovable? Well, some things we can approach with an attitude of "I could live with that" and others we approach with an attitude of "oh I love that". So, what makes the difference? How do we go from an attitude of I can tolerate something to a point or an attitude of, I love that?

There are many times it is totally associated with how we feel about something. Our feelings become bright and happy and joyous in any particular chore or aspect of our life from hanging out with certain friends to working our job on certain days or certain tasks that we might actually like. We love all the ones that we feel good about or in. It is interesting to think back or take notice of what you do on a day to day basis that you feel good about and the stuff you feel just plain old sucks. When we begin to notice things that we always have said "makes us feel bad" we can then begin to dig in to "the why?". There are many times it is our own outlook or attitude that actually sucks and not the person or the tasks we are involved with. Our own approach can make all the difference, we can tell ourselves that we will have fun doing something and then as if by magic it will be fun. If every person were to go through life just doing things that were to a standard of "ah screw it, it will do, I can live with that" then yes indeed life would become very grey all around us. Life is not grey though and quite the opposite, life is full of colour and vibrant, the word vibrant even, what does it bring to mind? If I say the word VIBRANT what is it that comes to mind? Colours perhaps or an idea of life? For me it makes an image of a happy person in my mind. Somebody who is vibrant, the person who is high on life, they might not be the most colourful though.

Does it mean we must have an overpowered passion for everything we come across in life? Not really, it would be nice to consider now that any tasks be it work or a chore at home, it is good to consider how if it is something, we are doing then perhaps we should do it well as it will always carry our mark on it. Our own fingerprints so to speak, the chores that we hate performing will be something that is associated to us personally. Should we do it to a standard of acceptable and "we can live with it" or can we do it to a standard of "oh I love it". For these reasons it is our choice to decide how we want to approach these tasks, it is our choice how those who view our work will either feel the livable nature in which we did it or the loveable nature. No, we are not doing this for the other people in life to comment or to be satisfied with, we are doing these things so that we will be happy with them. Any job or chore or task of any kind is not about the actual thing we must do, it is about us and how we do em and how we feel. These are the powers that we possess, we can change a whole day into a great day just by how we approach something and with what attitude is it that we go about our work.

We can do a day's work and feel horrible about it all and our only good pieces were lunch time and going home time. We perk up and feel good when we eat because satisfying our hunger is a nice feeling to have. When we are down in the dumps about our job or in our office, we can just become ecstatic when it comes to the end of a day because this is the time we leave and go to be where we are more comfortable. So, what if I told you it was possible to be happy all of the time, either at home in your comfort area and at work. It is possible to enjoy the chores and the tasks at work. Oh yes this is very possible. How?

Having an understanding why it is we do a chore or why it is that we go to work, what are these things for? I cannot know your job description so I cannot speak to the specifics of it nor do I know which chores you love and which chores do you hate. What I do know though is that it has absolutely nothing to do with the job or the chores, it all has to do with what you choose to say to yourself. Your approach to any situation is about how you decide to approach it.

Doing a good job is secondary to the actual doing of the job. It is a good thing to tell yourself you will do a good job and achieve this little item as the satisfaction attached can spark off some good feelings inside. Just to complete it can help us become happy. Completing something well, this brings a new type of satisfaction, similar to how we satisfied our hunger with our lunch but not exactly the same. It is in how we choose to be about the task, we possess the ability to like things and not like things. We have been figuring these out since we were a toddler. So, you might say right now, "hold on a minute I know what I like and don't like, that's simple" I say back, have you tried the things you do not like with a different attitude? Here is a possible way to approach. I have never been mad about doing this every week how and ever I am going to begin to like doing it even if it sucks. How about, I like to enjoy my day and so anything that comes my way will all be part of me and my world so it will be a nice day, I like nice.

Imagine a few simple words can change how we approach something and it can change how we feel about it and change the outcome of our own day. Just a few simple words to ourselves. That's magic.

Please do not take my word for it, please I ask of you to try it. Begin each day on such a positive note that even when we walk right into anything, we can achieve it, we can master it and we can enjoy it. These would be the differences between choosing to have a nice day and choosing not to. All within our own power

This leaves me to ask of you one more simple thing to consider. How do you see yourself?

Are you the masterpiece that you have been working on and are you the beautiful person you have always been? Then it is your duty to yourself to not allow negative thoughts to crowd your mind and dull your emotion. It is like as if you are worthy of so much more than you allow yourself. You deserve to be happy and making yourself happy depends on whether you think you are a person who is just livable or are you loveable?

When you find that a day is getting away from you and you are losing your focus to where it is all turning nasty and your feelings are turning sour, it is then at that point in your day, sneak off privately for like two minutes and refocus your mind. Do the breathing exercises and start over.

Begin again and regain the passion for life. Allow the feelings to pass through and reground yourself in your day. There is nothing that can change your day or make your day "shit" other than the attitude you carry with you. If you find yourself having a worse type of day, focus and regroup your thoughts and your emotions all over again. This is totally the difference between "nah I could live with it" or "yay I love it" all within our own powers of how and what we choose. I like to choose to enjoy my day, do you?

Operating within Society

When we find situations difficult to deal with, what do we do? Sometimes we avoid them because everything just seems a little easier when we ignore the things we find awkward or difficult.

I am passing on to you some small tools to use in your daily life, speaking to yourself in the mirror about how good you look. Telling yourself to accept the world and even the breathing technique that can change your whole way of being in life. So, what about the difficult situations. What about when we are overcome with some form of emotions that no matter what we say to ourselves it might not work. What about when we just plain old find things difficult? What can we do about those?

We must perform within society on some level or other, otherwise we would fall apart and cease to exist. So, we do operate within society and we allow some of the society criticisms to eat us up on the inside and we can often not come out of our house too often, so as to hide away from society when things just seem too hurtful to us. We might be super sensitive to the harshness of life and so it is, or we find it difficult. I cannot claim to you that there are magic secrets that I have that can take all anxieties away from you or make any pains go away, what I can do is let you know what I have done and that I have daily tools to help me through situations and things that can help my own mind remain focused. It is not an essential piece of our lives to have to perform well in the eyes of others nor is there any written document that says we must even participate. Society sets the standard of how we live; we follow along as it has been bred into us to keep on surviving and go forward each and every day. For some of us this may carry a stronger form of motivation in our daily routines and this would be why some of us achieve different levels than others. We already took a brief look at why some of us are just and quite simply different genetically and this can identify why there are in existence, different levels in life. We can look at nature and we can see the food chain as it may be called or look at the animal kingdom and see the food chain again and gain an understanding of "oh yeah, there are different levels, that is just the way it is".

So, what can make a difficult situation for us in life? Yes, things may occur around us that can be referred to as stimulus and so for this reason we become a person or the person that we are based upon what stimulates our own reactions and how we deal with what goes on around us. What happens? The stimulus triggers something in us, we react, or we respond in a certain way and this becomes who we are. We are triggered by all factors of everything around us. Actually, this brings me to a smile on my face because of the many in depth conversations I have with my great friend Wayne. These conversations can last a year sometimes. I claim that if we can find our inner self and we can be okay with how we feel at any given time then through basic relaxation and slight

meditation we can be very peaceful within ourselves.
Through staying in touch with ourselves in a clear and
conscious manner we can overcome any hurdles presented to
us and we do not have to be shifted in anyway by anything as
we can maintain an inner peace throughout any given day.
This peace is achieved by listening to ourselves and our
feelings. When we are breathing and feeling and our mind is
in a totally clear state, we can experience any of our feelings
and enjoy them. We can be sad but enjoy it as it is a pure
form of emotion and it passes through us and we begin to feel
better again as we have enjoyed a time of sadness all to
ourselves and it was pure and almost perfect. In this clear
state of mind type of living we can also help slow our mind
down from racing and our thoughts can become very clear.
Clear to the point that we become very aware of ourselves.
You could say to me that "of course I am aware of myself,
there is my leg, there is my foot, I can see my chest breathing
in and out" yes this would be an awareness of our actual
physical presence. The awareness of self I am speaking of is
being aware of what is in our mind, what are the thoughts we
are having and knowing why we are having these thoughts.
What are we feeling at any given moment and what is the root
cause or basis for how we feel? It is by having an
understanding of these kinds of thoughts and emotions and
the idea that our entire mind is made up of our brain and our
thoughts along with our emotional vault and our physical
presence that we can find that our complete person, the "who
we are" that it is this person that would be what I refer to as

"self-aware". And it is in this such state that I would suggest we can experience our life. My friend Wayne will present the debate to me that "that is all very well if we live in a vacuum" he presents to me often that it is or there are many stimuli around us that create a change to how we may actually be, by how we are perceiving and reacting to different stimulants around us in the world, be they actual physical objects placed around us or other people and how they are behaving. That these stimulants, "stimuli" even, are very much a factor of who we are and how we behave and how we often feel and think also. This would make a good argument for the case that we are perhaps two people many different times. One being the person we are on our inside and the person we fall asleep with every night when we lay our head on our pillow at night. The other person being the survivalist who reacts to all stimulants around us each and every day and how our own perception of life can be different from how we fall asleep at night. Our thoughts can be racing and our emotions all churned up along with a busy day based upon whatever it is that society will throw our way by way of stimulants. I have found that the stimulants are only as strong and as powerful as we allow them to be and that the vacuum my friend will debate with me is actually the inner workings of our self. We are the vacuum, should we make a decision to not allow anything outside of ourselves to alter our course or alter our mind in any way, then it is quite possible to remain within our vacuum of self and begin to enjoy our very existence.

What makes for a difficult situation on any given day?

I am totally aware that this question has no real correct or wrong answer as it is very much an individual thing. Each person is so different that really and truly it is no laughing matter. However, it is the similarities between us that keep us bonding with each other throughout life, there are some things that can be what we may call "common problems" that we can all experience from time to time. Although the answers to what may make a day difficult really is an endless topic, perhaps you can apply a little of what I mentioned as "breathing techniques" to whatever you find to be something difficult in your day.

Let's talk about our emotions being something that can bring about awkwardness and make something harder for us. Let us just say that we have always had a hard time with feeling anxious, our anxiety brings about changes within us that makes a day difficult. We have never known that it was any different for any other people and we thought that how we feel in our anxious moments is exactly how everyone feels. So, for this reason we never thought it to be weird or strange or anything, however we did find it difficult for ourselves. Anxiety can bring about a million thoughts a second, it can often feel like and we can begin even convincing ourselves of things that may not be correct based upon the racing mind that can develop while being anxious. I could say to keep it brief; our mind speeds up a little. Emotionally with anxiety we can turn into a washing machine on a fast spin cycle and we can go from upset and angry to paranoid and even laugh with speckles of joy thrown in for good measure too. Let us take a moment to break it down and see what may be going on, a scenario perhaps.

We walk down the street on our way to work, we are a little late, like let's say 2 or 3 minutes only. These 2 or 3 minutes can be enough to throw us into a spin. Some thoughts may occur like this, of course not everybody is the same but let's just use an example.

"they will all be there ahead of me, oh fuck! I better walk faster"

"why today the stupid bus had to be late and, on a Monday, too"

"I hate when everybody is already seated and awaiting the briefing before me"

"I am not doing Sunday nights at my sister's house anymore because I need to be up earlier and not be late for work"

"I am not even too fond of my sisters place and her husband anyway"

"I will never forget how he danced with me at their wedding. Drunk my arse, trying to cop a feel"

"she shouldn't be with him anyway"

"I bet he has cheated on her and what a dummy she is"

"I always told her to be more suspicious"

"that's why I don't date guys at the moment, too many of them wanna cheat"

"even the fella in our office, fooling around with the receptionist behind his wife's back, they are all at it"

"I bet I can even spot the ones who cheat walking down the street here. All prim and proper in their suits"

"why can't casual Friday just be every day?".   "I love my denims and trainers; I feel so comfortable in them"

"I could walk so much easier and wouldn't even be late if I had my trainers on"

"oh fuck, yeah! I am late. Shit!"

"I don't like being late, maybe I could just call in sick and say I don't feel well and go back home"

"they will all think I was drinking at the weekend and assume I just ended up with someone and am ditching work for a romp on a Monday"

"now my hands are sweating and if I start sweating all over, worst thing about rushing and having just hopped out of the shower" "will the landlord fix my shower this week. Why do I even pay rent when they are so slow to fix shit"

"I can't call in sick, I need the job to pay the rent to have a shower that doesn't work right"

"oh, I wish I could just escape it all and live on a beach"

So the example may seem a little humorous and is maybe a touch on the extreme but it is an example of what some anxiety can be like and how mind racing can occur and bring us to a very different area of thought all because we have a little awkwardness about ourselves and being late for work. An alternative to that could be in how we deal with or how we slow our mind down and use our breathing to help our entire mind focus. How about an alternative.

"oh, I am late, I will call and let them know I am gonna be possibly 5 minutes late"

"I had a nice weekend and it was good to catch up with my sister"

"I love my life and I need not worry about anyone thinking anything about me at my work. Late or not"

"Mondays can be fun watching everyone scurry past on the street in a hurry for work"

"I will enjoy my meditation this evening as it helps me focus on my feelings and the week has already begun"

So how do we change from ranting and raving in our heads to this calmer more enjoyable thought process? Basically, it is in how we can train ourselves to be more focused and in how we start our day. Using our breathing techniques can help us remain a little slower with the thoughts and help us to stay calm within our emotions and then our brain does not have to race off and have us going a full lap of the world with our thoughts. Staying in touch with our new Self and in our vacuum can mean we do not need to look at the people on the street as a bunch of cheaters and horrible people. We do not have to fear who is talking or thinking bad about us behind our back and we certainly do not have to have a full a to z of thoughts and emotions all in a 3-minute walk through downtown just because our bus was a couple of minutes late on a morning. How is this achieved?

It comes back to allowing or deciding to allow or choosing to allow our mind take over and run away with all kinds of thoughts. How can we stop it from doing that? Coming back to our breathing techniques. If we should like to try an exercise for 20 minutes, say 3 times a week, we can begin to get closer and closer to our own entire mind. We can train ourselves to slow everything down and only hear silence. We do this by finding somewhere comfortable and begin to breathe slowly. We inhale and exhale at an even rate and long deep breaths. You can practice for 20-minute sessions to begin to bring about a habit within your body that when you are breathing deep breaths and allowing your mind and emotions to focus on each other, then the habit is forming. Then through time, a 5 minutes session can be just enough to help you regain focus and become grounded. Before too long it can be a matter of one long deep breath that can allow you to bring you mind, body and soul all in line with each other and then the morning walking across town that you are late will be only a matter of one or two long deep breaths and the entire mind of you will get focused within seconds. Practicing this technique and developing it over a few months can bring you into an awesome place in life where no matter what the feelings or mind racing, or stimulus may be around you. You will be able to take back a clear and focused position within seconds.

We can lock on to drama in life too. This can be another type of mind racing opportunity and we can actually go out and about on our days seeking out some form of drama or other. Some of us actually thrive on the stuff and always have a way in which we can perceive a situation and take a more dramatic stance on it. If you are not like this as an individual, I am pretty sure you know someone who is, as there are loads of us in the world.

Why do some people seek out drama or try and change a situation into a more dramatic one? Hard to comprehend really if you cannot understand it, well it is as if the dramatic ones cannot understand what it might be like to not be dramatic. Again, if we think back to what might be stimulants in society and our lives, we might begin to understand that many items are all based upon perception. How do we perceive a situation? It is just like the 3d movies that come out from time to time. If we do not wear the special glasses, then we cannot see the movie the same as those who are wearing the special effects glasses. If we are not anxious and we are not dramatic then we cannot see things the same as those who are and of course this would also be the same for those that are dramatic and anxiety stricken, they will find it hard to see things from a more relaxed and calm perspective.

This then would allow us to gain an understanding that it is not what we see in front of us that is the same stimulant for everyone. Each individual may react differently to any given situation and so these are levels of how we see stuff differently. Yes, we are the same as far as we are human but that might be where the similarities stop. Why even mention this comparison or the differences between us? Because in fact it has been when I discovered this that many aspects and many reactions to different stimuli in my own life began to change. It has been how I have developed certain patterns for being and how I perceive any person or item, or situation is how I may react and how I may feel about something that actually matters to me. Another person can see differently, will feel something different and therefore more than likely react in a completely different manner. Having an understanding of this has brought about a great change in me and my own self.

So, what does that mean for living within society? How can we operate any differently within our society? One could argue that all we need to do is educate all those who are less knowledgeable, another may argue that if we teach by setting examples then others will come around to our way of thinking and the world will be a much better place for all. How and ever, perhaps we can look at some of the foundations that were laid within myself and see what tools I have drawn upon. As a young kid I gave up going to school and I went out on fishing boats and worked as a commercial fisherman. No not to bore you with fisherman stories, something I have learned as I have looked back over life is that at that time in my life, I was learning some valuable lessons. Our lessons are not always obvious or in plain sight. Often, we are learning inside our minds and we do not even notice at all.

Aboard the boats it is important to know the compass. The compass is a tool to know directions. N for North, S for South E for East & W for West. These are directions of the compass. I can tell you are making the connection already, yes you are right. So many people are in life "looking for direction" people want to know what direction they are going in. Many will say oh please don't give me directions to somewhere saying north and west etc., that they do not understand the compass. It was my early years spent fishing that I was learning the compass and the 360 degrees of the compass. There are 360 little tick marks all the way around the compass that each represents a direction. I will help you out a bit. You may have often heard, "oh they did a complete 180" that means they were heading north and then started heading south as south is represented on the compass by 180 degrees. Or some of you may have heard, "he did a complete 360" 360 degrees are the complete circle, a full turn around and return back to where they were going anyway as North is represented by zero and 360 on the compass. That is the full circle so to speak, well there are also all the other little numbers representing other degrees on the compass that I was learning too. When aboard a boat, it is a good idea to know where each little degree is and what is it's opposite also. I was learning about all of the degrees of the compass which then led to later in life understanding things from many different angles and viewpoints, at least 360 of them. Understanding the compass by default has led me to view things from side views and reverse views and different angles of all around the full 360 degrees. It is this idea of perception, how we see things and then hearing from others that has helped me to be able to see things from a different angle and begin to see another person's point of view and or their perception so to speak. I am not recommending to you that you change your own view points about anything, what I am suggesting is beginning to have an understanding that not everyone sees things the same as you and many times people will not understand your own view point and this can lead to many frustrating situations. It will be hard to change someone else's perspective or viewpoint and so the easiest I have found is to try and see the other person's view, this is an easier task than trying to change their viewpoint or convince anyone of another angle to see things from.

To operate within our society requires of us some patience with others but most importantly with ourselves. Not reacting to stimulants around us and being able to refocus our mind when we feel the need to. Taking those breaths and training our entire body to know that a deep breath can bring us right back to grounded. Seeing other people's perspective can make things so much clearer for us that we can save ourselves the time wasted on frustrations. We can train ourselves to be less dramatic about any situation and allow ourselves to be less frustrated in any drama though nobody may see our point. We can however, we can begin to find ways to see the dramatic persons viewpoint.

We can save ourselves from anxious moments by learning methods and ways to remain calm and we can and have the full ability to choose how we are going to act, react and what way we will deal with our feelings.

Being able to view another person's perspective on any given issue can bring great clarity to life and lessen our headaches on a day to day basis. Learning to focus our mind and clearing it mostly can bring to us great perception and this coupled with a multi angle view can increase our own awareness of ourselves to where life within our society is something, we do not have to avoid at all. More so we can enjoy it to its fullest capacity. Whether or not we are one person when we rest our head for the night alone with our own thoughts or a person who is overanxious and having a racing mind, we can definitely bring about the same calm into our everyday living. We can be a complete person inside and out and within our day, all day.

These are important little factors of becoming self-aware and leading to a much calmer type of living and it is with these kinds of small adjustments to ourselves we can not only cope with society, we can definitely live within it, quite well. No matter the situation, no matter what it is that life wishes to throw at you. Your own ability to slow it all down and realign your thoughts and allow your feelings pass through you can be the difference of getting through it or getting annoyed to a point of frustration that all hell is breaking loose. Altering you angle of view around any situation can help you gain clarity and peace of mind.

Just a couple of simpler pointers to maybe assist in how to operate within society. Other people will most certainly have a different viewpoint, and this is totally fine. It is also fine that other people do not wish to even look at it from how you see it. It is upon ourselves to adjust to how we see it that will help bring about a clearer picture of anything for ourselves. Ourselves are what matter and rather than become frustrated or overanxious, our own ability to shift how we see something makes life within our society an easier time for ourselves.

Remembering that there are possibly 360 different angles to view any one situation from. When we allow ourselves to take a little different angle of view, we can then begin to see a how or a why another person may act in a certain way. Understanding these other viewpoints can make our own lives a little more stress free.

After all who is it that matters most?

Yup, ourselves.

RELAXATION REMEDIES

Many of us can have a hard time finding the time to relax and then when we finally get a moment to ourselves, we cannot even begin to relax as the moments have become few and far between. We do not know what to do with ourselves when we get some down time or alone time. What can we know about relaxing when it has become almost foreign to us? We do know that we can listen to some music or maybe you are reading this book right now as a form of relaxing. As here again based upon our many differences as humans there are several different levels to find some relaxation in.

When a week of work has left you feeling tired and even a little highly strung, finding the stress levels hard to turn off or slow down can be a difficult place to be when it comes to Friday evening. The weekend looming and a whole host of activities planned and all you have is Friday evening to unwind a little and take some time to try and relax. How can one just simply flip a switch and go from 9 to 5 go getter businessperson or Monday to Friday delivery driver to relaxed weekend mode? It is a great question isn't it? Trying to find something that works for yourself can be difficult in our modern times. So many friends are always quick to tell us what we should try and how they find great relaxation in blah blah blah. I dare to ask you; do they really get relaxed though? They are indeed easy words to speak and people will tell you they are relaxed just so as to not have you pry into their real feelings. It's all part of that mask we wear out in public again.

It is normal and part of everyday life for us all to wear the mask and as we mentioned earlier, not to want or just naturally have no desire to be our true own self out among the public. There are those of us who can find ways to relax though and it doesn't matter to me if I am in public or at home all by myself. I will just mellow out if the setting is right, to be fair though, I didn't just have that ability all by myself. It did take a little practice. I can recall being invited to go to a symphony one evening and yes it does sound a little out of the norm of things to do on a Saturday evening, but I went along to check it out. I sat there in my chair listening to the music and before I knew it, I was out cold. Well, not out cold exactly I suppose if I am to be honest, I was in a state of limbo so to speak. I can recall how I was unconscious to the world around me, the symphony hall and all the people in it, I was involved with the music in some sedate way. It really was like magic. When the orchestra were finished it was as if I was waking up from a deep sleep and I was asking my friends, had I been snoring or anything? I felt like I had been asleep. I wasn't asleep though; I was in a trance and a complete relaxed state where only the music was happening for me in my mind and all around me. What I have since learned from this encounter was that it is possible to sink in or slip away with soft music even at home. You can try it for yourself and see will it work. Find a comfortable seat and close your eyes while allowing some music to play. Maybe pull a curtain or dim down some lights and just allow your body and mind to concentrate on the music only. Listen to the music, try and see if this can be something you can do for an hour on a Friday evening. It is like a form of meditation where becoming one with something allows the entire world to disappear for a small time and the entire mind, that being the feeling part and the thinking part and your physical self all joining together in sync to enjoy some moments all to yourself. Any good relaxation is always just on the edge of asleep and awake. No thoughts in the head and soft calm feelings from the gut, magically really.

There are those of us who might not be able to slow down the mind on just our first attempt and we may need a little practice at it. This is totally okay and keeping in mind also that there are no right or wrong ways to relax. It is a "thing" that is very much individual and for this reason it is worth trying out some of the stuff your friends will suggest to you along your journey in life. Just try em, if they do not work it is okay. Not everything that works for another will work for you. The fact you are willing to try suggests to me that you will find what level you are on and where your own relaxation remedy actually lies in life.

Going to the gym and working out can be a great way to finish the week off and my special time has always been in the swimming pool. My routine used to be to enter the gym and dive straight into the pool. I would swim an uncounted number of lengths, most often until I can begin to hear my own heartbeat in my ears, that was my marker to slow it down. I would then roll on to my back and float along, kicking

gently to propel myself down the lane and watching the
ceiling of the pool house. I would use my hands to flap a little
and keep my straight line and just chill. Having your ears
under the water helps block out the other noises and floating
aimlessly along the lane of the pool has been a great way to
relax for me. There is something in the keeping my ears under
the water and kind of forcing the brain to switch off due to
less noise, I guess. The tiniest of little panic can occur when
you have an instinctive feeling that the wall must be close and
you are about to bang your head off of it. The panic is natural
and not enough to bring about anything major, it does help me
feel and be aware of myself. Floating in the water has another
piece to it that I guess is something to do with the body
becoming very relaxed and happy in a sense. Floating
weightless eases stress and allows me to just be one with the
element of water and thoughts from my mind can flow away
as if to leak into the waters around me. I have found great
benefit from swimming, plus it is a great way to be working
out and keeping fit also. I will also admit that after a swim
and a little time spent floating on my back, I head for the
sauna usually and once there I again focus on my breathing
and allow myself to slip nicely into a state of relaxation.
Another 15 to 30 minutes of being at one with only my
breathing and allowing my body to completely turn off. The
benefits of relaxing this way have brought great feeling to my
entire mind. I always know when I am not in a good place to
relax when I cannot slow the noise of my heart beat from my
ears while floating or I cannot stand the heat of the sauna

room, these are signs to me that I am not able to relax at those times and so I usually go and sit in the pool with my arms resting on the side and kick my legs slowly through the water to help tire them out a bit and then I will try again the sauna.

Swimming may not be your thing and I totally understand too, however if you are willing to try it, you may find some of the great relaxation values that I have found over the years.

There is nothing wrong with pampering ourselves a little bit every so often either. Ways in which to do so can be as soothing as going shopping and buying ourselves some new bed sheets and pillows. The art of shopping itself can help bring about some feel good feelings. Just the simple act of buying something for ourselves can have a great, well not achievement but satisfaction attached to it. Buying ourselves a little treat, the relaxation side of it can be how we just wander around the shops in no particular order or on no particular schedule. When we buy our self some nice new pillows and sheets there is a double bonus affect because when we go home and dress the bed and finally fall into our nest to sleep, ah yes, this can be so rewarding. We can melt away again in a nice new hotel feel to our own bed. I recommend finding the highest thread count you can find for the sheets; you will be glad you did when you feel how soothing your night's sleep can be. This is just another form of how we can distract ourselves with an activity like shopping and take some relaxation from it. With again the double bonus of relaxing into nice new sheets.

Another I have found quite powerful is the spoiling ourselves in a different way, massage. Yes, this my friends is a therapy designed and by its very own purpose, a relaxation method. It can be a little expensive to find a good masseuse and it is hard to justify spending money on ourselves with new sheets and nights out at the symphony. Answer me this then, are you not worth it? Do all your work and hard weeks not make you feel you deserve to spoil yourself just a little? Try it and see. Find the best place you can for a massage and set out to enjoy it. Allow yourself to slip off into a nice dreamlike state of mind as the massage takes care of your muscles. Taking care of our muscles is a great way to give them a little thanks for doing our walking and carrying us around all over the place. If you think about it, we give very little thought about how much our body actually does for us. Yes, we make some decisions to eat a bit better every now and again and to try and be nice to our body. Nothing is nicer than a long soothing massage. This would be another time of half falling asleep and just simply relaxing. Although it might not be for everyone, I do highly recommend it as it is a nice way to give something back to our body and we get to a relaxation state of mind by allowing the massage work for us, so another double bonus right there. Isn't it funny how we can spend money on many less or more like trivial things and when it comes to ourselves, spending money on an expensive massage seems to be too expensive? It is your body and we do not have any replacement ones so I can only call it money well spent.

I can remember one time where I went to a spa type hotel and it was all about relaxation. I looked at the menu for the treatments and options available for me for the weekend. Checked in on a Friday night and had a few snack type tapas for an evening snack. The room had a little self-catering available so the next morning was about making up a light lunch before the spa treatments. What spa treatments did I choose? It was a location where there were natural springs all around the hotel because of volcanic waters and hot springs. I chose to have a mineral bath and a mud bath followed by a massage. The total time for the treatments were set to be about 2 or 2 and half hours. Seemed a short time considering I was staying for two nights. So, after a light lunch and some time spent floating in the pools I headed for the treatments. I was taken and shown the baths and did the mineral pool treatments and then the mud bath and off to a massage room. Let me just say that it was an "absolutely fabulous" experience and something everyone should do at least once a year. It is as if an entire layer of my skin was scrubbed off me or something, I mean my arms after it felt like they were someone else's, smooth and soft and like I had just had all new skin applied to me. My stomach felt great and my entire body and most importantly I was super relaxed. I do get it that it might not be for everyone, it is just another sort of relaxation remedy I found extremely useful. Having a mud bath was a new experience for me and it did feel a little weird at first, I can tell you honestly the weirdness didn't last too long and the results afterwards were amazing.

It is important that we look after our body, mind and spirit if we are to take relaxing seriously. Many will say it is not easy and they never can find the time to do anything for themselves, then if this is the case, stop and slow everything down. Find room in your schedule to pencil in a few dates that you can whiz off to a spa and be pampered. You deserve it. Remembering of course that if we do not relax our body and we do not slow down our mind we are just forcing ourselves to move closer and closer to our grave where yes, we will end up anyway, but it will be nice to go there knowing we have been very nice to ourselves and our body.

As a man it is a different story to be heading off for spa days and taking time out of life for massages etc. etc. I found that heading to a salon for men is a great way to pass a few hours. Get a haircut and a beard trim is a nice soothing experience and if they have massage available then choose one every so often. Get a pedicure, allow someone touch your feet and cut your nails etc. These things are all great ways to recharge the batteries and formulas for a very successful week. There is nothing more powerful inside of ourselves than feeling "on". This energy that comes out of us when we are at our most relaxed is almost something others can sense from us and they tend to stand back and almost like allow us to lead the way for us to continue on a very successful path in life. It is something we ooze when we are relaxed. Our happiness is so raw and natural that people are ready to lift us up to meet our goals. All of a sudden and for what seems like no apparent reason people are helping us. The roadblocks of life just seem to shift out of the way and we can master anything. This is all very possible and very amazing to experience and feel. So, when you are "on" you are ON!

I have given you some of the methods I have used and why they are or were important to me. The key piece of it all has been peace & relaxation. Getting to a stage in our lives where relaxing is actually important. There are so many ways in which relaxing can help our bodies, the body needs some love and care and some mellow out time. It is through relaxing all of our organs that the stuff inside of us can work just a little better and with so much more ease. Ease is a great word to think of right here. To take it easy would be an expression to suggest relaxing. There is a key element to the opposite of uneasy, to suggest at ease. I present to you another word which is worth consideration in regard to relaxing and why it is very important to us and our body, Disease, yup Dis~Ease. There are many readings and writings on disease and stress related illness that I hope you are taking note of the point I am making here. Disease, think of when you get a dripping nose or some flu type infection. Many will ask you if you are feeling run down, are you down and in a bad place emotionally right now? Bags under your eyes from not enough sleep perhaps? Sometimes we can get these little white blister type things inside of our mouths on the inside of our cheeks for example, they say it is a sign of being tired or run down. It is in these times that other types of infections seem to creep in and grab a hold of our bodies. This marks the importance of relaxing and taking care of ourselves. In order to help begin on a journey of finding ways to relax, a super key element is to work on our own sleep pattern. It is very important to ensure we are getting enough sleep and even though that late night snack or an evening meal which is a little too late in the evening, even though it seems like a great idea, it is wise not to eat too heavily before bedtime as our body will continue working on processing everything we just ate while we sleep. We may wake up the next day and feel like we just got no value from our sleep. This can lead to a down type of day just from simple tiredness, which then in turn can bring about some infection in our body.

As an alternate to this of course is the feeling good and being upbeat and fresh for any day. Having had plenty of sleep and feeling good, it makes sense that if our body is easily run down by lack of sleep or lack of relaxing then it is very simple to make the connection to our mental state of mind and how clear our own head is. When we are lacking in sleep, we can present physical ailments like the white blisters inside of our mouth. Another tell-tale sign of this is tiny little white pimple type things that can appear just below our eyelids. These little white pimples are tiny and can be hard to notice but again a sign. All of these being tiny signs of the possible onset of something worse can be due to lack of sleep.

When we are emotionally drained and lacking in ability to feel our emotions it is also possible to become down and is

142

another time when disease and infection can creep into our life. So emotional health is as important as physical. When we are avoiding our own feelings, it is possible to become constipated even, this type of physical lack of system working can again bring about disease inside of our body and so it shows us how important emotional health is too.

Relaxing plays a massive part in how we develop and continue in our lives. The physical benefits are massive and I suppose the obvious "go to guy" when we think of the benefits of relaxation. Where we may forget to consider is our emotional health as well. The benefits of relaxation can be equally important to our mental health also.

RELAXATION

Important for physical health. Avoid disease.

Important for our emotional health. Avoid disease.

Important for our mental health. Avoid disease.

Three very key reasons to take a serious look at relaxing more in your lifetime.

We can pamper our body and feel really well. A good massage can help relieve any constipation even, just like we do when we are dealing with a newborn baby and we can massage their little tummy to help them pass what they need to do.

We can soak ourselves in the bath tub with awesome music playing or attend the symphony and be one with the music, this can release emotions from our body and help from being backed up so to speak and help us maintain an emotional and physical health balance inside of ourselves and in our life.

So now it only stands to reason by process of association that relaxing and being at ease versus the process of being not at ease and the possibility for infection from disease. It is then very important we give some thought to mental health as well. Freeing our mind up to allow us the moments we need to feel and the moments that we need to feel physically well too. Seeking out a balance where it would allow us to feel good, feel at ease and feel super fabulous in our own (new) skin.

All of these are wonderful, what if we cannot slow down our mind long enough to allow ourselves slip off into the music? What if the steam room at the gym is not relaxing to us and what if the mud baths or the shopping and sleeping in new sheets are just not enough and not allowing us to chill and relax? Why are they not allowing us to do, what is keeping us from half falling asleep during an expensive massage? Our mind.

Yes, our mind can prevent us from enjoying any exercise we might try as relaxation. So, we move from one form of relaxation that a friend suggests to the next and never find any value out of any of them, we scroll the Internet for relaxation ideas and every time we try one of them we just never seem to grasp the concept or the feeling of being at ease. The mind, our head, our mental health is preventing us from taking it easy. Our thoughts will not slow down for long enough to give us a chance.

What can we do about that?

Something I have tried for many years now and I have found it to be very good. I do not need music and I do not need a weekend getaway to a spa resort either. Nope, I need to breathe. I need to allow my breathing to be so focused that the only things on my mind or in my feelings are the here and now of my breathing. When we breathe deeply and take some time to allow our mind to clear we can really begin to feel the benefits of our relaxation. We can begin to sleep more and much better too. Our breathing is the key or a key to trigger everything to work for us. I know it sounds funny when you attend a class or a talk of any kind and the speaker or teacher says, "now I would like you all to take in a deep breath & release". Something so simple as our own breathing can bring our mind down from all kinds of dramas and circumstances we have been concocting inside of our minds. Inside of the mental part of our mind, we can stay totally focused on 4000 thoughts a second inside of our head and we will find it very hard to gain benefit from any form of relaxation. I have tried the pampering and the shopping and massages and the music. The single thing that I have found most beneficial to all departments was to train myself to breathe.

The breathing is slow and deep breaths in and exhale the same. We can train ourselves to just breathe. Nothing more, just breathe. It is a nice practice to train ourselves in to and a great way to become mindful of ourselves in all aspects of our mind. The physical element of breathing is massive and beyond what we might think. Scientifically our breathing is helping to bring in new oxygen which in turn goes to our muscles and helps them work. The breath we take in helps fill our lungs and then the lungs distribute blood with oxygen all around our body. Practicing our breathing is a difficult enough one to get a handle on and yet we do it all day every day. What is the difference if we are breathing every day and we are still stressed and always ill?

I say, try breathing and only breathing. Try breathing for 20 minutes, in and out slowly. Sometimes as I breathe in, I will tense up some of my muscles, starting down at my toes and through my feet and on up to my legs and so on and so forth. It is through this time while breathing I will tell myself in my mind that as I breathe in, I am delivering new oxygen to my lungs. As I think the thought I can feel the air filling up my chest area and as I release the breath and exhale I relax my muscles and allow the exhale to carry out all the toxic stuff in my life or what may feel like a pain or two inside of my body. I try to bring myself to a relaxed state by just focusing on my breathing. I focus on how it feels coming into my body and I also focus on the "crap" that occurs when I exhale.

If we can slow down our breathing to a snail's pace we can begin to feel. There is nothing more satisfying that feeling relaxed through our own breathing and seeing as you pointed out earlier of how we are breathing all of the time, I would say that yes we are breathing but are we taking deep breaths and enjoying each and every one of them, is it possible that right in the middle of a breathing exercise that we may start to feel emotions begin to slow as we relax each muscle as we exhale. I find that getting a massage at a spa may not help my mental health. I find that being emotionally involved with music might feel good but not allow my mind to clear and relax.

However, I find that breathing and practicing my breathing actually helps balance all three. Sometimes as I do my breathing, I find all my muscles getting a little break and feeling better. I often times also feel well and feel new feelings come up and float away again while I focus on breathing. These connections are amazing really. If we can by combining all three stimulants together and spend a day at the spa getting pampered and we find ourselves too stressed for the sauna, then perhaps a breathing exercise will be the simplest one to achieve and help align our feelings with our thoughts and it is then that we can relax in any of the methods I have used in the past, meditative breathing is something we can all do.

There are no membership forms to sign and no money out from the bank either, not expensive at all, just find some quiet time to yourself in a quiet place and practice breathing.

When we practice deep breathing exercises over a twenty-minute period we can begin to form a habit inside of our mind and body that will help us become calm & allow our mind to clear. When we have developed the habit, we can cut our times shorter if needs be and we can grab five minutes here and there catching a few deep breaths to help calm us at any given time in our day.

When we have mastered the habit and developed it within ourselves, we can then even get to two or three deep breaths at any time when we feel our mind becoming a little rushed or cloudy. We can bring a pause to our life for up to one minute which can help relax us immediately. How can we go from majorly stressed or an over worked mind to just one minute of breathing to calm ourselves? With practice is how we do it. We can train our entire mind and every time we stop for a pause and realign ourselves; we can reap the benefits.

It is the least expensive method of relaxation we can ever sign up for and in my own experience the most effective.

I am totally not saying we should not try a few of the more expensive treats for ourselves from time to time but the simplistic is so natural, cheap and amazingly, it works.

Here is a pause moment to allow you to breathe, take 5 minutes and relax.

BENEFITS

What are possible benefits to any of us of trying to bring about some relaxation habits into our life? Can it really be worth it to try and seriously try and slow our life down to some breathing exercises and all will become magically wonderful in our day to day world?

I suppose we would need to look at what we call "benefits". Are these something that represents to us an advantage in the game of life? There are many people we will come across in life that will never do anything for anyone unless they can see a clear benefit to themselves. Some of us will call people like this selfish, as there always has to be something in it for them, we might even avoid such people as we see their game and we do not wish to play in it, if there is never any good benefit for themselves. I try not to judge any other person by how they operate within the game of life. It does not unbalance or affect me in any way, if someone is caught in their mind to have to always win outright then that is their issue not mine. A real question I ask myself is, does it really matter to me? Another question I ask you right now is, how do you see the word benefit? What does it mean for you?

To some people the word benefit can automatically relate to money. To others the word benefit can mean gaining something as in a position in life or gaining some free time. For example, we opt in to sharing driving our kids to different activities and then when it is someone else's turn to drive our own kids we can say "it is a great benefit to have the evenings free when it is the other parents turn to drive" so benefit here would be we gain some free time to do other things We can see how being part of different groups in our own social circles can bring us great benefit by having some very solid friends to be able to have time with and share stories or confide in and so having such friends can bring great benefit in to our lives to help us have outlets to pour our hearts out and help us get a little balance. Having good friends is a great benefit to our life.

I guess the word benefit has a selfish tone to it too as it is not just a night out attending the blank blank benefit night in aid of someone else. Like all words it can be how we use them or what they mean to us ourselves that can determine how we move through our day. If I were to abstain from social gatherings because I see no great benefit to myself, I might become a hermit of sorts or a recluse. If I were to not do random acts of kindness for others, then I would be pretty boring I guess all because I am hell bent on finding the benefit to me element. So, what are benefits? How should we seek them out and what should we do with them?

If I am in receipt of a benefit from another human in whatever circle it may be, the parent's group or my social network or a dear friend who allows me whine and spill my guts about all that is wrong in my feelings, should I gain from them and never return the favour? Perhaps I can go through life looking for everything that is of benefit to me and to hell with anyone else. This would be pretty selfish alright.

Ya see it does come down to how we determine what the actual word means to us ourselves. Just like the genetics and the differences we possess in life; it is probable that we also hold different viewpoints of what any one word means to us as individuals. We can read the word,

BENEFIT

And it may mean so many different things to so many different people. Of course, yes that can be said for all words and how each individual interprets the word. So, it is for this very reason that I must ask you another question. So far, we have glanced at ideas of receiving benefits in life from groups outside of ourselves and I have discussed about receiving money or time or things again that are outside of ourselves. The question I have is,

In what way do you benefit yourself?

This is a very real and honest question I would like you to ask yourself. Please pause for a moment. Here is a little space on the page if you wish to doodle down some answers.

Have you come up with anything yet? Let us take a look at some especially since we have just finished up a chapter on relaxation, it is topical to remain on the idea of what it is these relaxations actual do and here we are going to discover some benefits that we may have been neglecting for quite some time.

If we associate benefits with outside things and people outside of ourselves, well it is time to change these thoughts. Let us go back to the wheel of the compass and begin to view from a different angle. Let us look at the angle of how it is possible that through our OWN work on our OWN self that we can be in receipt of massive benefit in our OWN life.

Stuff that does not have to cost us money and does not cost us anything really. Yes, there is time we must spend working on ourselves, but this is not a cost. The time spent working on ourselves is a benefit. This is a new angle to take for sure. Yes, up until now it has seemed like taking time to practice breathing would be something that requires finding the time to do it, this has equated in your mind as a cost. Finding time to do anything for ourselves seems to equate as a cost. The new angle of view to take is to see this as a benefit. Should you wish to prove me wrong then this would mean you would have to try some of the stuff I have suggested and then come back and tell me I was wrong and it has cost you too much time. I, however, am confident that once you set out to prove me wrong and do actually try some relaxation that you will find the benefit and then the debate would be settled. So please do not take my word for these things at all, try them and see.

Being good to ourselves is probably one of the simplest things we can do. When we were born and as a toddler growing up, we amused ourselves. We might not remember sitting in a little carry type seat and flicking at a brightly coloured key chain and little clown figurines that were placed across the carry bar of the seat, but chances are we did. We flicked at it and we were focused on just that bright coloured object and nothing else. We flicked it and it moved and we laughed. That seems pretty straight forward and simple doesn't it? What it shows me is that when we did not know anything about life and the world, we were able to enjoy ourselves much more simply.

How can we have moved so far from the simplicity of when we were a toddler? So many adults act in many childish ways and annoy the living hell out of one another that it really is not funny at all. So how do certain childish things stick with us and others seem to disappear? Where has the innocence of our days of just rolling around on the floor and playing with coloured shapes gone? What would happen if we decided to be so childish and just lay on the floor and roll a ball for a little while. Would this mean us mad? Would we be able to focus on only the ball and the floor and nothing else? Why would we do something so silly if we do not see any benefit in it? Can we still feel the magic of staring up in the sky at the stars on a clear night and only our thoughts drifting off in to outer space, is it possible to bring back some of our childish thoughts to help us focus on just one thing and allow our mind to clear?

We have been entertaining ourselves since we started out in the world and as we have grown up, we have sought for things (stimulants) from outside of ourselves to continue to provide joy to us. Are items outside of our self really necessary?

Yes, we can gain nice feelings by having a nice evening out with friends or a loved one. We can join a team and play sports and on the evenings that we go to practice, we benefit from being around our team mates as well as gaining from a physical work out. These carry great benefits to our personal life. We can offer ourselves to our friends to help them through a rough patch and be that ear of friendship. This can be a great benefit to them. All of these things are awesome and well worth it. What about ourselves?

Can we take another angle of view, let's imagine the compass again and we will look from a different viewpoint perhaps?

Investing.

Investing in ourselves is a way we may understand it a little better. Let's take the selfish aspect as a starting place. I want to get the maximum out of life, yet I want to spend the least. How can we figure this out? How about we say or use the clichés. You get out what you put in. If you want to put in the least, then it makes sense that perhaps we get the least out. This of course again is quite general and is about stuff that is out there outside of ourselves. The idea of using the compass to come from a different new angle is to look inside of ourselves. How much are you willing to invest into yourself to gain from life?

How can I invest in myself is a probable question you have right now too? And it is a very good question, what this question does is mark the beginning of starting to invest in yourself.

It is different for each of us, it can mean changing the meals we eat, what time we eat them and what type of foods we are putting into our body. It can mean that we intend to invest in ourselves by creating comfort around our own life. We can and I would highly recommend that you invest in expensive bed sheets and a very comfortable pillow for your bed where you sleep at night. There really is no reason that your own bed at home should not feel like a 5-star hotel suite. Why? The place where you sleep is where you recharge yourself for each new day in life. Doesn't it make sense that the highest comfort to sleep in could help you gain maximum rest and then feeling refreshed every day in your life is a great step in the right direction.

So, once you have the bed linen sorted out, more household items to invest in are luxurious towels for yourself. Yup just like again at the 5-star Hotel Spa for example. Every day you step out of the shower it is highly recommended that you wrap yourself in fine expensive towels. You may have always thought that reasonably priced bed linen or cheap enough towels are just items and not very important in life. If it were to be that towels and bed linen are not important then there would not be such varying differences in prices when it comes to such items for your home. If we can get a refreshing night's sleep and feel totally plush in our towels after stepping out of our morning shower, then we can actually mow down any obstacle that shows up in our day. Feeling right is a huge issue that is probably the most important piece of a success strategy we could ever have in our life. Imagine a set of sheets, a good pillow and a nice set of bathroom towels and we can begin to become a powerhouse in our daily lives.

Can we invest in ourselves without the cost of cottons? Of course, we can and it is probably the most important piece of all. Teaching ourselves the techniques of how to RELAX. We will gain benefits in our life from nice sheets and towels, yes. The more important piece is can we slow our body and mind down to a slow enough pace that we begin to see everything clearly? Is it possible that by becoming more aware of ourselves that we can find our level in life? Again, the answer has to be, of course. But how?

Invest in your breathing techniques. Begin to find the time on a daily basis to switch off from your everyday world. Switching off for 20 to 30 minutes per day. Once a day or evening. Allow yourself some time to sit as relaxed as you can with no other distractions. Be with yourself for 20 minutes per day.

*Focus on how you breathe. Pay special attention to how your thoughts work to make attempts to distract you. Pay more attention to how your own muscles have little aches and pains and that by taking this time to relax is giving them an opportunity to flex and relax too as they need it.

*Allow your mind to slow down.

While practicing slow deep breaths, allow your mind to focus on the way in which the oxygen enters into your nose.

*Feel how your chest gets larger as you breathe in, feel how the body is thankful for taking the little breaths it needs.

*Focus your thought on each breath as it enters and stay clear in your mind that with each simple new breath comes new life to your entire body. Each muscle that has been slightly neglected through the day is now getting the time it deserves and is able to fill with new oxygen and can begin to relax.

*As you exhale feel the nastiness of your day leave your body, mind and spirit each time you breathe out.

*Leave negative feelings escape from the inside of you with each breath as you exhale.

Now that you are beginning to feel relaxed and your mind is slowly becoming less foggy and a clarity is creeping into your life, this will be a good time to focus on your body.

*As you inhale beginning with your toes, curl them a little as you breathe in.

*Bring in the new oxygen all the way down to your feet.

*Squeeze just a little your toes as you breathe in.

*As you breathe out allow your toes to stretch back out and relax as you breathe out. You are now working your muscles of your toes in sync with your lungs as they breathe for you. Try two nice breaths in and out using the stretch and relax of the toes with each cycle of breathing.

As you take in the air feel how the toes are squeezed slightly and even hold the muscles and the breath for a single second and then exhale while allowing the toes to stretch out again.

*Now move up to your calf muscles and repeat the same exercises, breathe in and squeeze up your calf muscles as you do, hold a second and as you exhale allow the calf to loosen and begin to relax. Repeat two or three times.

*Our thigh muscle one of the biggest in our body. Again, breathe in slowly and steadily, you can bend your knees a little for this as squeezing the thigh is helped by this.

*Breathe all the way in and hold, breathe out and allow the muscle to relax. Repeat two to three times.

If you are sitting down for this exercise it will now be the joyful piece of squeezing your buttocks as you breathe in.

*Again, as we breathe in new air and new life in to our body, we are squeezing our buttocks to hold just a second and exhale as we relax the muscles again.

We are becoming more conscious of our own body now. We are becoming more conscious of our muscles individually. These breaths each time are still carrying all the good energy to our entire body and our muscles are beginning to relax.

*Focusing on our body will allow us to notice our chest moving up and down with each breath. We can feel our own stomach now as we breathe.

*We continue breathing in and out slowly and with each breath we are experiencing new life in our entire body.

*We can now squeeze a little our stomach as we breathe in. And as we exhale, we allow all the feelings rush out from our body. We breathe in again new air and feel our stomach clench with the new air.

*We exhale all of the horrible things we have felt for our day and we relax our muscle as we do so.

*It is nice to lower our hands down by our sides and begin again our little stretches by beginning down at our fists. As we breathe in, a tightened fist and as we breathe out, we relax the whole hand. Repeating only twice or three times and allowing our arms to hang by our sides.

*We again focus on the forearm for some more breathing and muscle relaxation.

*Up to our shoulders and as we release our shoulders on exhale, we can allow our neck to slip to one side.

*Roll our neck around gently as we breathe in and out. Drop your head forward slightly and allow your neck to rest.

If you wish to invest in your life, invest in yourself. Then you will not find any excuses to perform some of these exercises as often as you can. Light soft music can help set the mood too. Sometimes it can be difficult to begin as the mind is too filled with fog and gentle music can help break down the noise in one's head.

By practicing the breathing our mind can begin to clear and become as refreshed as our whole body. Do not rush to jump right back into chores or any other exercises. Allow the 20-minute relaxation you have just done to work its way through your body.

This is what I call a massive benefit to ourselves in life.

Coupled with a nice pillow and comfortable sheets, the sleep you will now have will be like getting a full make over. Waking up each morning after investing in your own relaxation will definitely be a way in which you can head out into the world and win at the game of life.

So, taking a little time for ourselves and allowing our mind to slow and become clear can be the difference of a good day and a great day. The difference of feeling up tight as opposed to relaxed is like night and day. What did it cost you? Where was the big cost in investing in your own life?

You can be very clear about how you will proceed in whatever tasks you have in your path this new day. All from a little self-investment.

Now those are what we can all call BENEFITS.

What is talk?

Sometimes when we do a relaxation session for ourselves and we can find that feelings just come up from like out of nowhere. No forewarning and things we didn't even know we might be feeling. There are times when some feelings are just a little trapped and when we practice our breathing, we may find ourselves becoming a little emotional. This is totally "normal" and fine too.

If I were to know exactly how I feel about everything every single minute of the day then I probably would not have time for much else. I guess we kind of all have a little strategy inside of ourselves to cruise on through a day from time to time and have no awareness of self. This would be considered "normal" and we can rest assured there is not a single thing different about ourselves from any other person just because we might have some feelings lingering inside of us. What can cause this type of trapped feelings can be anything from old habits that we thought ourselves when we were just four or five years of age for example. There is a possibility that we tend to go into our own head space from time to time and can spend time unaware of what might be going on for our emotional self. The good thing about any of our feelings is that whether we are feeling them, or they are a little stuffed inside of ourselves, well nothing in our feeling life can become too big and consume us completely.

There are times that I am steam rolled by my own emotions and I mean steam rolled. I am totally unaware and I get into some breathing. It can be any time of any given day and when I slow down my entire life and what I am doing for the benefits of concentrating on my breathing and then boom! Feelings of all kinds of things can begin stirring, I mean I can become so needy and feeling vulnerable that when I feel little tears begin to run down my cheeks that I do not even want to see myself in the mirror so I do not have to see a vision of how emotional I actually am at that time. I can feel even physically a little flutter or two across my chest and my breathing can begin to lose its rhythm. Usually these are when I have been keeping to myself too much. Times when I am completely alone in my thoughts for say the duration of a week. Alone in my thoughts and feelings to a point where I am not going insane or anything, but I may not have checked in with myself and I may not have been too clued in as to what might be going on for myself. Again, just to make a point that becoming emotional for no reason is not at all in anyway anything wrong or any reason or excuse to run off into a mind frenzy panic of "oh my God! What is wrong with me?" If you have ever found yourself in a place that I am talking about, well you are probably just experiencing a very human thing happening. Something many of us can experience in life and many times in our lives too.

Then what is talk? And what can talk have to do with any of this?

Cliché again, "no man is an island". What does this actually mean? Of course, no man is an island as an island is an island and a man is a man. Very simple yes?

We humans have a funny thing somewhere inside of us that causes us to want to be around other people. Even when we say "I want to be left alone and I do not want to be around other people" did you know that I have found that it is at this time that we probably are wishing to be around people the most. Now if that is not confusing, well what is? lol

We have funny little mechanisms inside of us that will do a lot of hard work to convince ourselves that other people cannot take away our pain or other people do not understand us. So why even bother trying to explain? Who really wants to hear about our shitty little problems anyways? While we do consider other people's feelings in this respect, sometimes we need to be selfish. Be selfish to cater to our own needs and allow our self to pour out all of our problems, pour out all of our grievances about life and our work colleagues or our families. Give to ourselves the gift of not caring about anything else except allowing ourselves time to pour it all out in a good old fashioned "chat" with a friend. This is an exact use of talk that can be of massive super benefit to us in our life.

Taking some time to be selfish in this regard and talking with someone about our problems as we see them. We do not have to talk with anyone as a way of seeking advice or a way to use another person as a sounding board. Sometimes we need to just talk. Talking to someone can help us realign things inside of our own mind and can have huge benefit to how we can allow our little tiny trapped feelings to come out a little and help us deal with them.

This is a great answer to a fine question of "what is talk?"

Talking can help us in a number of ways. One of the important ways that I have found is that if while we are talking, have you ever noticed that you actually hear your own self speaking. We hear our words and just by talking with someone else we can catch ourselves mid-sentence and find a solution to whatever our issue is. This is why I would encourage everyone to talk to someone. Be it a family member or a loyal friend. Possibly you have more than one family member and more than one friend. To begin talking with someone or anyone we do not have to build up to it in any way. We do not have to schedule someone and be on edge or in any way apprehensive. Talk is a gift given to us to allow us to dump out some garbage sometimes. We need other people from time to time to offload, dump or get off our chest some, finding a path to our happy place inside of ourselves. We can use talking to help us get to the bottom of our own feelings and another person can apply how they think about our situation, sometimes even giving us great advice.

Talking is a way in which we can grow. By hearing ourselves sometimes and how we speak or what we say when we are talking can often help us give ourselves some very good advice too. What is actually going on between two people amidst a "talk'? Is it an equal flow of speaking and then listening, one mentions something and the other listens, then they follow up with their stuff and a little piece of what they think about your situation? Sometimes when talking with someone they actually might not be listening at all. They may be so caught up in their own issues that hearing all about your issues, well there just isn't any more room in their locker for your crap and theirs all mixed together. This is by no means an excuse not to talk with someone. Talking can bring about so much deep and meaningful stuff for any individual. Talking is a way in which we can dig inside and bring up those stuffed feelings. A way in which to help you justify your position and purpose in the world. Talking can be about many other things too. We might talk for business for example.

Our job might require us to teach or give sales demonstrations in front of large groups of people. We may need to take time with our own relaxation and healing in our life when our talking needs to be about our own inner workings and not the rehearsed speeches we give for our job, yet it is all talking right? So, what changes between discussing a plan for a new construction project and chatting with a friend about a horrible embarrassing situation that happened to you during the week? What changes or what is the difference between talking to a colleague or a schoolteacher about our children's performance in school and talking with a therapist about our day to day struggles in our lives? All of the items are about talking, some for a living as in a "job" and others are about talking about ourselves in an effort to dig through our emotions and find where we sit best with any particular issue we may have at the time.

Can we take a safe position and say that talking about ourselves feels a little uncomfortable and giving a sales seminar can be just more simple as we have no emotional attachment to the talk, this type of talk is from our head and we can do it in our sleep, although discussing our feelings is like giving a stranger the pin number to our atm card? It might also be safe to say that when we talk with a friend or family member about our issues that we may be doing it in such a way that is our hidden piece of ourselves that we are sharing and due to the emotions attached we are more vulnerable to any remarks, criticisms or otherwise. In talking for our job, we may just be using words we have practiced over and over again with no emotional attachment at all.

Perhaps the title of this chapter may have been better titled, "Talk what can it be good for, in my life?"

We can talk to our children and be like a teacher, educating the little person, helping them to understand something. This can be quite emotional as there is a huge possibility that while we give this little life lesson to one of our little persons of the world, we may actually be influencing their little lives. We may take some time to talk with a child and while doing so, again we can hear ourselves speaking. We can or might hear the absolute sense that we are making and we may be teaching ourselves a little trick or two too. We thought we were helping a little child although we might be helping ourselves too. These kinds of talks are a great way to enrich our own life and the lives of others around us. Fulfilling might be a fair way to recognize some of why the emotions are feeling so good when we do these kinds of things through talk.

Let's get back to the island though. We need other people though. We need to take our chances that the friend we have chosen might not fully understand us and after we expose some inside truths about ourselves to another human being, we can begin to feel scared that another human knows about how I feel. Oh boy, should we hit the panic button. I guess it is only proper and very fair to mention that there are some of us out there that do not have a loyal friend or we have never felt close enough to another human to be able to find a safe ground between us to begin discussing our inner self. Therapists may advertise their services as a safe environment. A friend may express that their door is always open, or their home is a safe place to talk if you need it. Sometimes some of us may actually never shut up talking and when there is nothing to talk about, it is almost as if the person invents stuff to be overanxious about and then Boom more talk.

I will say I have found it always very healthy to talk with others. Speak out about concerns, share feelings and encourage others through their tough times that they might need some talk too. All this can be achieved by talking.

Some stuff that flies around the Internet these days are posts here and there about "just talk" talk so that others can be able to offer advice or help.

Talk to help ease any of your concerns or issues. They say, "A problem shared is a problem halved". I will agree with this also. Sometimes there is nobody to turn to and just chat and blurt everything out. Sometimes your friends have become well used to you talking about things that they no longer hang on your every word. It does not matter if you have a position like this one as talking about your issues is a selfish act and is all about doing it for your own benefit and not for theirs anyway.

To those who feel like they have nobody to let it all out to, there are trained professionals who will help you go through your feelings and just chat with you. There is absolutely nothing wrong with this. There is an awful stigma attached to how if people are to seek out a private therapist that they must have something wrong with them. I say to this, nah that would be rude to say. I say fair play to any of you who have sought out therapy and are making tracks forward by having somewhere to talk. To those of you who might be reading right here and think that I know you and this sentence is for you, well it is. Talk to a friend, a neighbour, a teacher, a therapist, a helpline in a confidential manner, if you ever feel that you cannot handle your feelings. If you have ever found yourself feeling so intensely that you begin to believe your own feelings might actually consume you and cause horrible things in your life, then? Yes, you have guessed it. Talk!

Build up enough courage and reach out. Nobody will ever judge you for bringing up a tough issue. No one will ever listen to you so intensely as to take every word you say on board and be able to remember precisely as they will have their own things going on for them within moments of you sharing with them. Talk to anybody maybe another great heading for this chapter as it holds great truth in it.

If you ever find yourself in a tough emotional place in life, please do understand that talking can help. From the little tiny emotions to some of the big ones. Talk is something I think we could not do without in our life. Find time to talk to other people, find time for yourself to sort through your own feelings. Talk through the ideas you have and some of your own preferences about life.

When a car begins to make a little funny noise, for a short time we ignore it. It becomes worse through time and we now say that "we must bring the car to the mechanic". We too are like the car with the little noise. When our mind begins making a little noise inside of our heads, isn't it fair to say that even if we ignore it for a while, the issue never really goes away? We can probably say the exact same process as with the car. After a while and when it gets a little worse through time. "get to a therapist and talk out some of your stuff" just like the car and the mechanic, our mind body and spirit can need a little safe haven to talk. You would not expect your life to run perfectly and be fixed because of a therapy session. To talk and allow ourselves to realize the benefits of talking is a major win in our life and we can do it at any time in our life.

Yes, you are right so many things are so "cliché" and yes you are also right that you have heard many items that I am writing about here before. As a matter of fact, you may have even heard of them all before. The point is that hearing them and knowing them are two different things, implementing them into your life is a whole new step and perhaps now this can be the last time you just hear about them and now you can just begin doing. Start talking today is the best advice I would ever be able to give anyone about anything. So many of us have feelings deep inside which we have buried. So many of us feel like nobody wants to listen. So many of us find it hard to find a person to be so comfortable with that we can tell all to. So many of us think that if we expose ourselves to another human being now, they have stuff on us and can take us down should they ever wish to.

Yes, they are all valid reasons for not talking more often and not talking about how and who we are. It is time now to say screw all that nonsense. I am going to talk about myself and my feelings because I want a better life for myself. I am going

173

to talk with someone to begin to ease my worries and my frustrations in life. I am going to begin talking because I am worth it. Remember it is for you yourself that you begin to talk with another. I know it can be painful when someone comes up to you and when you actually tune out slightly and all you can hear is, my this and my that. Me, me, me and I did this and I did that and I, I, I. Though it may be a tad painful to listen to what we are not noticing about this is, that person is looking after themselves and they didn't even know it. They are offloading and dumping, they are beginning to feel great about themselves, all the while we are in the conversation too and we are a little dazed and confused by them. We are muddled up with our own stuff and we have no chance to jump in and begin our little rant of my and me and I. The time today is a great time to start and begin to look after yourself just a little bit, begin to talk. Start off with some small stuff and build up from there.

I do not know you; I cannot know you until you make yourself known to me. I cannot just say that you are this type of person or that type of person. I cannot know what you go through or any specifics of your life. I have no clue. What I can say is that whoever you are, you are human just like me and I do not wish for any other human to ever have to hurt inside all alone. I can also say with confidence that I am happy you are in this world and I hope to someday meet you. I wish to enjoy the value you bring to your own life and the world. These are the reasons I say to you, do not allow some built in mechanisms hold you back from the great you that you are.

Push aside the defense mechanisms and begin talking to others. Share your issues and get on a journey of being nice to yourself by offloading some of the mixed-up crap that can go on inside yourself on any given day. Allow yourself to feel your way in this life. It is beautiful and can be so rewarding.

You do not have to take my word for it, begin talking and see for yourself. Just another simple tool to help any human being along the journey of life. Be good to yourself by allowing self to come out and play. Introduce yourself to your friends and all of us too.

NEW LIFE

Now that we have gone about considering some relaxation and some talking, perhaps it is time we can have a look at what a "new life" might be like. It is one thing to begin using some tools and some different thought patterns to enrich our lives and help us become more balanced as people. So, what do we do with all this new fun energy we have created inside of ourselves? What is this transformation in our world and what are we going to do with our new and improved self? Our new life.

It is fair to say that our life does not really become new or we do not just automatically start living a new way. There is no switch to just change the channel overnight. We do however begin to change slightly and over time. Can we reinvent ourselves? Is it possible that all this change that we have spent so much time in fear of, is it possible that we can overcome our fear and actually begin a new life for ourselves?

I happen to be living proof to the world around me that I can have a new life and have had great change in my own life. I have endured some horrendous times in my life and I am here writing this book to hopefully reach you and let you know that it is very possible and it is a wonderful thing to be able to get to a new level in life and enjoy some new approaches and new thinking along with all the wonderful stuff that exists in the world.

What is a New Life?

Some of us move into adulthood and we begin to have children. These little babies show us what and how new life is so much fun and so amazing really. How a baby grows and watching how they have their own little instincts as soon as they are born. We see new life.

We go for a walk, in winter and we notice how things are quite dull and grey. The hedges by the roadside are all dark and have been soaked by the rains. It is the same roadside that we can walk in springtime and we see the green leaves and the berries beginning to grow. It is possible for us to see new life be born all around us in nature.

Nature is a wonderful example of how we can see what a beautiful world it is that we live in. Sometimes I will go and sit by the coast and lookout as the birds fly across the ocean. They sometimes fly at what looks like only a few inches from the top of the sea. I can look around and see the cliffs as they drop down to the pebbled beach and the waves landing on the shore. The fields around and the plants all growing up towards the sun. This big fire ball in the sky that somehow as if by magic gives to plants life. Not too long ago actually I spent about an hour in a local park. As I sat on a bench I listened, I could hear the wind. I could hear the air and the bird's songs, many different birds all singing slightly differently. Their chirps were sounding like happy birds. The shrubs and trees and hedges were swaying a little from the breeze and the whole place was alive with new life. I saw bees moving from flower to flower, they do not seem to pick just one type of flower, but they do the same routine. I know we all heard of the "busy bee" and really and truly if you take a little time someday to sit in a park you will see them working away tirelessly. As with all good nature programs and documentaries we are aware that this is new life and it is all around us at all times. Do we have the time in our busy life to stop and enjoy it?

New life is wonderful when we stop and take it in and begin a small appreciation for the amazing planet we live on. I can tell you of many of the amazing sites I have seen in my life which are some fantastic things and maybe you can say it is easier for me to have gained such an appreciation because of my own travels around the world. I have found that even the simplicity in sitting by the beach or in the park, all still has as much going on no matter what part of the world you are in. It really is about us allowing ourselves the little bit of time to enjoy it and pause our whole busy life and take some time in nature. New life is everywhere and it is beautiful. Perhaps you can agree?

Soooooooo. Or the big BUT.

What happens in our lives that we fear change so much? How is it that becoming our own true self seems to be so hard for us? Allowing our emotions to come through and allowing our mind to relax and be the person we have always been. This brings about fear and we fear change. The evidence however is all around us. The evidence of how new life is absolutely beautiful, yet we fear to begin our own new life. We have grown from child to adult and we have learned many new things along the way. We have become conditioned, well somewhat, by society and we have a fear of changing ourselves. We can carry fear of being our self. Again, the clichés or what you may have heard many people say, "change is scary", "I am not sure I like this new me", "I fear letting go of the old me".

All relevant and all very real for any individual. The busy bee does not fear anything. He may get eaten as he works his way around the flowers of the day, yet he is just being him. The birds singing do not care where they will eat or where they will sleep, they just keep chirping away. It is in nature all-around of us that and I say again, that nature and new life are some of the most beautiful things ever to happen. The trees and hedges and all plant life look so bare in winter but when spring comes around all kinds of new life springs up and sprouts out from everywhere and these are very beautiful indeed. It only makes sense that we allow ourselves to become who we are and sprout our own new buds of life and begin new life ourselves without any fear.

Turning over a new leaf it is sometimes called. The page in our book, in our story a new chapter begins. There are many ways to look at it and there are many reasons that our society on a whole is responsible for conditioning us into thinking that making changes and beginning a new life is a scary thing. These are things we have heard and concepts we have been led to believe in that change is scary, these ideas or ideals of the world in which society operates says or identifies that humans find change a little scary, some may clam up and cannot break through and others will never even consider a new way of life for themselves as it requires too many things to change around them.

Now let us take a different look at life around us, let's forget about society for a moment. If we sit and listen to the bird's song, we can hear something of joy in their tone, we can take a cliff walk and notice how the seagulls have eggs in their nests. We may happen across some new lambs in the fields in spring bouncing around all happy. Have you ever seen a new little foal when they are born? They must stand up immediately and they do and when they discover that they can run and what their legs are for they bounce around like crazy, bucking and leaping with joy. We stand there willing our newborn child to finally take a first step and go from crawling to walking. All on their own two feet, we have watched them struggle and crawl around the floor for months already, but they have seen us walking so they instinctively and by watching us all of the time, they want to stand upright and walk too. Isn't it a precious moment when your children take their first steps? This is a big change for them, they go from having learned about the world in their early months in life by having an angle of view from down on the ground. We pick them up and we carry our babies around on our hip from time to time and they must really like the view and how things look because they do not hesitate and without fear they change their angle of view; they stand up and they begin a new life for themselves. A baby has not been seduced by society and led to believe in anything. There has been no understanding or long period of time where a baby has seen and heard that change is scary, a baby knows nothing of such fears and will continue to grow and change. So, what happens inside of us, the adults? Where did we learn these fears? Ahh the answer perhaps is in how we feel. Our feelings tell us to be scared or our feelings feel too muddled and confused about change is an excuse to stay stuck where we are. How can we overcome such fears? What are they and why does it feel so weird to begin on a new part of our journey in life?

I suppose it is fair to say here and again that I do not hold some magic wand or have any formula that makes change any easier or any theory as to why it all happens the way it does. I can only offer to you an angle of view that may help you understand something different and in the hope of giving to you a new outlook or perspective to make things a little easier, that's all.

Scenario.

Something needs to change in your life and the time is right. You must move on from "friends" you must change how you live; you must change the people you are involved with and you find you must break out a little and let yourself grow. These things would suggest you are just like the tree in winter and have been in a slight hibernation type state of mind and it is now time to grow new buds and allow yourself to begin to flower and stand tall with some amazing mite, all the while looking so beautiful and to be fully admired. This is new life. For me I have had these kinds of things happen in a few different times of my life.

Let's just say a person, not particularly you but if it fits then okay. Let's just say a person is a drug user. Not a class A type drug user or for want of a better term "crack head" let's just say they indulge somewhat.

We now refer to this as "recreational drugs" the term itself is showing how society has begun to accept such things as drug use, "recreational". So, a person has been using drugs for quite some time in their life. Their drug use has not caused any social problems thus far and there has been no need to enter rehab or go to therapy of any kind. The person plods along and goes to their job every day and is a performing person within society. The drug use however is considered illegal. They must hide their recreational habit. They must meet people who are drug dealers from time to time to "score" and they must make certain moves in their life to hide many aspects of their drug use. They have done this for so long that it is all just part of their normal everyday life now. Going to the atm and making sure they have the cash for their stash, smoking slyly by themselves or popping pills when no one is watching all in an effort to stay "high" and continue to function. They function at their job without problem but they always have in the back of their mind that a day that might come around and they are randomly drug tested will be the day they just quit anyway, so as long as that doesn't happen, they will just keep on using drugs. Society says the drugs are bad and not welcome in the workplace. Insurers will not extend coverage to companies with drug using employees and so the drugs are definitely shunned by society, from the top on down.

Can we ask this person to give up the drugs? Will they just listen to us and say, "yeah sure why not" or will they fear the change in life so much that they will cling on to their drugs to their grave? This same person is a fine employee and is never late or never has a bad report from any clients and so they are a good employee. I guess the point here would be, if you are a good employee as a drug user then would you ever consider that as a non-drug user this person might have the chance of being a great employee. Perhaps this same person is a good parent and manages to do everything for their children. They perform well as a parent and are able to provide and do good things with their kids. Again, I suggest that the possibility to be great exists if we take away the drugs. Why will someone not go without? What is it that they fear? What is it about making a new start in life and becoming drug free that holds this person back? Imagine, no more hiding and no more preoccupation about having the cash on them ready to score the drugs. No more meeting illegal people and performing illegal transactions. Imagine.

What is it that this person is fearing? At the moment they are living in an underlying fear of going to jail. They constantly have an underlying fear of being caught out by their job and they continue daily with fear of it all falling apart by perhaps one random drug testing at work. That is a lot of fears if you ask me. Enough fear to say that because they have carried the fear around with them for so long that they have become accustomed to it. Yet there is a fear of changing. A fear of allowing themselves out into the world and meet the people on a feel-good basis without the drugs. Some people will use drugs as a way to cope with society, some will only feel comfortable when they are high. I say to this that there are way more good times and experiences and feelings to be had without the drugs & that it is 100% worth trying the No drug way of life. This would be my own personal opinion based on my own life. I said no to drugs as a 17-year-old boy and that was pretty much the way it would be from that point forward. It was back then that I learned about change and feelings.

So, what happens to this person in our scenario? There must be some major piece of themselves that they do not like, or they are unable to be comfortable about allowing themselves out into the world. What is the fear about taking on new life?

People may see me for who I really am, this could be a concept that exists. How about people may begin to see you for the great person that you are. I suppose it is also fair to say that for every excuse that a drug user can come up with for why they use drugs there is a counter argument that would suggest things can only be better without them.

People do not understand me is another that is something I have heard many times as a reason not to hang up the auld druggie bag and try a new life. "Nobody gets me" is one that is another great cliché of a person who uses drugs to allow be the blockade that will prevent them from making a change. I argue back that how can people "Get" you if they have not had the privilege to actually know you. If you remain hidden inside of a different type of persona and do not allow the real person of you out to meet us, then how can we ever "get" you. Ya see a whole new life awaits this person who has been using drugs as a coping method for so long. A new life just like all of the nature I have mentioned before. The tree that will shed its leaves in winter and begin again with new life in spring does not need to represent itself as a pine tree in winter and a great oak tree in summer. No, the oak tree remains an oak tree all of the time, but it goes through some change. There are cycles to life, there are times when we will be down and be less of a fun person to be around and then there are times, we will be upbeat and all kinds of fun. These things are all normal parts of living. If we are hiding our true self from the world then we must ask ourselves why? What piece of us have we developed a mechanism of hiding from everybody and why? What piece do we wish to keep buried and what has society told us about this piece of ourselves that we are not okay with?

New life is about us, inside of ourselves. The person who we were born to be is the most perfect person we could ever be. The beauty we possess as a human is just like all of that which is in nature around us and just like how many of the general public will appreciate nature in its beauty, they will appreciate us too. What we may think are bad pieces of ourselves or "negatives" can turn out to be positives and what all of society has been waiting to see of us for a very long time. The fear of the drug user about how they could actually cope and live without the constant state of being high. The fear of change and the different person they will become. "I do not wish to be depressed so I stay high".

Any person can say that they have a fear of being judged by their peers and so for this reason they keep little bits of themselves hidden. Just like the drug user here is the same thing, keeping things hidden. When we fear being judged by our peers it is something inside of our own mind. I am not saying that our peers do not judge us, what I am saying is that it is a concept in our minds first off. It is ourselves that is doing the judging first.

There are no requirements for any person to change so it is not like you must change your ways or your life. What is happening though is that everything around you and within you is changing all of the time. Just like nature in springtime it is not that you must fear any such changes at all but recognize the beauty in yourself and welcome the changes. Appreciate the changes in yourself. See how the changes are only minute and that it is all about the real you shining through and letting all the rest of us see that the real you, is very beautiful indeed.

A method or mode of how we can become okay with these little changes in life is by finding a way in which to talk about them. To talk with someone is the most valuable gift we can have. The ability to communicate to another how we feel. The ability to help ourselves to shine through, sometimes we might use talking to explain ourselves to someone we care about and they may not get the point exactly but it is not for them that we do the talking, it is for ourselves that we help come to terms with the little changes or corrections that occur within us and around us to help us become the great person that we started out in life as. It is by talking to others that we can let them know the who we are and the what we are and of course the why we are. The most important aspect is that when we are talking, we are very much listening to ourselves and although we may not have a full awareness that we are hearing ourselves speak, we most definitely are. All the time we thought that talking was to share our experience of our feelings and our inner secrets with others when all the while talking is a way in which we can digest some of what we have to say.

It is therefore important that when we do find some courage and a little strength to start sharing things about ourselves that we become okay with our own voice and that we are not scared of telling another but perhaps a little scared of hearing how we actually talk out loud about ourselves. This would give good reason to learn and chose our words in a way in which we hear ourselves say nice things. We use nice words.

Some simple things we can say are how we see ourselves and what beauty we possess. Using the right words can teach us by us hearing them and what we say when we are talking is hugely important to how we might successfully change our life around and begin again in "New Life".

A new life or new lifestyle can bring about wonderful things for us to enjoy. We have but one life to live and we can keep changing it and make changes to everything around ourselves and all the different groups of friends we may interact with along the way. We may have even had a few different close partners in our life to where we never really got back to the basics of who we are.

This one life that we have been given since birth is something we can toy around with and tweak a little here and there all the time. We can bring about in our world new life to ourselves. Our journey of discovery all about ourselves can be something or somewhere in life that we learn all about ourselves piece by piece every day. It is possible to change things around and to conquer our fears. But what fear really? Fear of letting other people really get to know the you that you are.

The you that you are is wonderful, beautiful and perfect all wrapped in to one super person. Allowing that person shine through is the best new life we can have.

Like I was saying earlier I learned about myself and turning over a new leaf and a new life back when I was seventeen. Things I have learned since then have been amazing. The one real thing though that always crops back up in my mind is how society has placed many expectations upon us as human beings. There are many concepts of living we must adhere to and try to be. Oh, what pressure. I say to you that try as best you can to understand that there is no exact way in which you should be. Be the person who you are, no other person will judge you for being you. The very same you who might think you cannot be yourself and cannot tell others about how you feel or what you feel you are becoming; it is the real person inside of yourself that all others will truly love. Do not hide or have any hidden ways to cover up and keep from others. Let yourself out, taste this new life you breathe every day and bring it all back to those basics we were born with.

No problem or issue is ever too big not to be figured out and with any of the labels society have are only for those who buy into the labeling concept. You are the best and perfect you. Allow the rest of us to get to know you from time to time. We would appreciate that.

New life can mean so many things and we are all deserved of new beginnings. When we find ourselves becoming more baby like perhaps this is the time that we are ready to begin again or take on a fresh start. Remembering that the baby does a lot of crying. Perhaps a good cry every now again can help us through our new start in "new life".

GRIEF

I suppose the simplest approach here is to tell you about myself and some of the journey of why I write nowadays.

The nuts and bolts of it are that I have changed my life in many ways as I was growing up. I was explaining this a little earlier. Did I grieve the drugs and alcohol when I gave them up in my teenage years? Probably but not in any real memorable way. In my adult life I have had two very traumatic experiences to do with losing my two sons. Darra was 15 years of age and he did not wake up for school one morning and that was that. Sudden death is what they have called it, he died in his sleep. Patrick managed to walk his way to a swimming pool at a very young age of 1 year and 4 months old and he drowned. I tried to perform mouth to mouth to revive him and it simply did not work. These are some of the hard facts about traumas that have occurred in my life. I have been living with grief for some time now in my adult life as I miss my children. To explain what this grief is like can be very difficult to describe sometimes but here is an attempt. Maybe you can relate to some pieces, maybe not. There is no one correct way in dealing with or living with grief. So, if we do not seem on the same path in our grief then it is still okay too. Just as we are individuals in this world, so is our grief a very individual experience.

From the moment I first learned of Darra dying I had feelings come over me of absolute rage but at the very same time extreme sadness. The tears flowed from my eyes and I somehow managed to make the longest and most difficult flight of my life to return home to see my son in a coffin. This has been such a horrible memory and piece of my story that I carry with me and it is only fair I share it with you as to allow some of myself out to you. I did not know what to think or in which direction to look on the plane home. It was an 11-hour flight and all I could do was cry and feel my lips as if they were swollen and trying to mumble but it was just muttering and mumbles of hurt trying to come out from deep inside of my gut. I was full of anger and I had no idea what would face me when I got to his house. What I did arrive to was a wake and my beautiful baby 15 years of age in a coffin. This kind of thing, nobody can prepare for and is not something I could ever wish on my worst of enemies. I do not know if it is like they say, that losing a sibling, or a parent is a different kind of hurt and that losing a child is just a harder or more difficult to understand kind of pain. I can definitely say and say very clearly it is one hell of a pain to work through.

Within a couple of quick years of having my head up my ass or in some form of buried in the sand, I did become a father again and my new light in life was born. Patrick, the most beautiful of babies and he would bring to my life some hope of being able to grow from all the pain of losing Darra so young in life.

Patrick's death was horrific and just as traumatizing as Darra's. Nothing can split them inside of me to say I loved one any more than the other or of how it just plain and simple hurts to miss them. The grief can be unbearable sometimes and it is these two children of mine that have inspired me to write.

Their dying has led me on a journey of digging even deeper inside of myself to begin to gain a snippet of understanding. It is basically why I have compiled much of my thoughts and explanations into this book to offer insight to others who perhaps have not begun to scratch the surface of their own grief and for those of you who, maybe, who cannot see things the way in which I do now. It has been immense pain and grief that have led me to an understanding of life. A kind of way of how these two situations have forced me to go even further inside of myself and see how my feelings and my thoughts can influence and or be a hindrance to my actions and this would be at any given time on any given day. Right now, it is possible that you are scratching your head a little bit and saying "wait A minute here, go back, did he just say, buried his two children and traumatic experiences" hold up a second.

Yes, I did just drop the bomb out there on you. The whole three years that occurred from December 2011 to July 2014, those few years saw me go from being a happy go lucky kind of guy who loved life and had put many situations behind himself from an earlier "misspent youth" type stuff to a complete and utter shambles of a man. Beat down by life, trodden on by the so called "winds of change" if you like. You may have an understanding of what it might be like to have your world turned upside down due to some life altering event. I am also aware that there are many out there that understand trauma and what it might be like to go through such severely shocking stuff in one's lifetime. I can only say, "so tough". I have or could never imagine the whole thing to happen again. When I speak of horrendous or horrific experiences, they really are understatements although they are quite drastic words to have to use, ever.

My grief has consisted of a lot of questions and limited amounts of answers, there is just nobody to ask. The pains that can bring me down as a person and hurt like all hell and the thoughts that can begin to drive me to an almost point of no return have been very real for me. So, this larger than life word GRIEF gets thrown around a lot and some often mention the "stages of grief" and at what point one may be at in their grieving. These are all nice ways of looking at the concept of grief and what it might actually be, our feelings are definitely taken to a new level and how the feelings and thoughts can combine to stay so focused on the actual negative that has occurred can swamp the living daylights out of a person. I am a true living survivor or person dealing with this kind of stuff on a daily basis.

Like I said, I have had the misfortune of having to bury my two children on two very different occasions and for two completely different deaths. The similarities, both are my sons, both had graves to go in to and both hurt like hell. So, what does grief mean to me nowadays and what do I do?

Here are some suggestions or ideas based on what I have found out to be, well what I might call simple remedies. Nothing can fix the way it is or change things to go back to how they used to be. Nothing will ever be the same again. It is a hard thing to understand if you have never been through it and it is even harder for the person living in it to explain.

My son's deaths have led me to look back in my life and try and find a why? looking for some signal to how this all may have come about. Not soul searching, just more like asking myself "what is it in my life that twisted or turned in any particular way that led me to where I am today?" The answers were or have been limited and my questioning does continue.

What I have found in my look back over my life was that not only are my two beautiful son's deaths somewhat unbelievable but a whole bunch of my life and the ever-changing nature of it has been pretty unbelievable also. This led me to make notes and begin writing things down, my experiences and some of my travels and adventures. The end result of this, I wrote a book "TWO sons TOO many".

Why mention another book of mine in here? To self-promote (yes of course) but to demonstrate to you that within my grief and my hurt and out of death, something new has been born. A monument to my children. This book has become somewhat of an amazing journey for me, every time somebody tells me they are reading my book or sends me a message of how they have just finished my book, I smile both inside and outside. Another person has just read all about me and my inner feelings and my life. The beautiful thing though is they have shared a moment of mine and paused to imagine Darra and to think of both Patrick and Darra and this somehow gives me a tiny tiny bit of comfort. I did not know the first or last thing about writing a book or the business of books or publishing or any of that type of thing. TWO sons TOO many exists and is out there and I am now an author. Another life change that is just part of my story as it continues.

What makes me proud of my achievement in this book writing stuff is that I was totally beat up from life, I really didn't think I could change again and reinvent myself as a person anymore. The death of my sons has been the extreme of hurt and pain. Writing has been a formula to help me set goals in life again. Little goals where I can set myself a target to have some chapters finished by certain times of the year. I have taken to advertising my writing and books and built a website to showcase where I write some short stories and some blogs. I have all my social media accounts now set up to help me advertise and attract new readers all to read some of my writing. It has been of inspirational value to readers to read about my story on how I have picked myself up time and time again in life and turned it around. Some readers find things motivational as I have demonstrated to the world that even in the hardest part of my journey a new direction was born, and I continued on. These are the important pieces in my grief that may help another out there who has their head hung low. I too was at the end of my wits to find out how can I live again, how can I love again and how on earth will I ever laugh again. It is possible, I am living proof that the journey did not end with the loss of my children. Yes, the story completely changed and yes that life today has been more about finding solutions to problems and taking a basic view of almost everything.

It has been my breaking everything down into simple parts that has helped me see more clearly. The breathing I have mentioned earlier is a technique that has brought me to a clearer viewpoint of any issue that may raise itself up in any day. These are the tools I have been recommending to you because, well quite simply, they work. It is from learning and teaching myself to understand how I hurt and what the feelings really are that has helped me to become okay with all of the pain. I now enjoy it, which I know sounds like something sadistic, but it is that I prefer now to be real and I know that my pain is authentic. What is a better way to live than to feel every little bit? Just now as I feel good days and enjoy the fun and laughter it is just as real when a day is a little more down and reflections of the past come to haunt me so to speak, these too are real. I have grown hugely appreciative of real and authentic feelings. I have learned to see beauty and I have also grown to see things in a basic light.

With all the stresses and anxiety life can bring about in a day, it is how I have brought things back to a very basic practice for myself of allowing my body to breathe in the air that I need. This is my most basic need in life, to breathe. From this foundation I / we can begin again and start our day over. We can begin to figure out some of the most complex of our feelings and we can grow into the person we are and have always been. Understanding a tree in nature or understanding another person's motives or agendas all can stem from knowing our own feelings and practicing our breathing.

I am not saying that everyone who grieves should become a writer and spread the great word through books. What I am pointing out is that a project of any type can become something in where we can express ourselves and set little targets for ourselves and we can actually meet our goals in our project and take great satisfaction from this.

We can remain in our feelings "in the now" and enjoy them, though it could be argued that we endure them as the feelings in grief are quite cumbersome. It is the rawness of the feelings that were so new to me. I had been living a feeling type of life for many years and I had no idea things could ever get so raw and gritty. And look at me, a man over 6ft tall and full of muscle, a fine specimen of a man. I always had a presence when I walked into a room, I walked tall all my life (might have been called an arrogant asshole a few times too lol) how and ever I was beat down. I wanted to be left alone and not noticed. I avoided conversations with people and I walked away from wherever I felt hurt was happening. This is where grief was taking me. To grow out from this to have my little projects and then speak to people about my grief and this was brought about because of conversations about my books. Interviews and radio programs and group talks all born out of the hard path because of my loved ones no longer being around for me to have fun with.

I found out the hard way, it is us who have to make our own fun. It is upon us to make our own life and it is entirely us who can create a life of misery and being down just as much as it is upon us to lift ourselves up and keep going forward regardless of what shitty hand, we feel we have been dealt. Yes, it is a fine thing to wallow for a while and feel like we have been hard done by, of course naturally, I have lost my children and anyone who grieves has lost someone near and dear to them also. So, it makes perfect sense to wallow for a while, the piece of our thoughts running away with us and bringing us down is a tough one because it can be hard to claw our way back up out of it. It is why I believe in setting goals, small short-term goals that we can achieve. There was once a time my goal set was to get out of bed and be sure to take a shower for the day. Get up and start the day, I promised myself I must shave and be clean, when I would catch a glimpse of myself in a mirror and realize I was beginning to grow a beard, well I knew I hadn't been hitting my goals. I had to break life down to a very simple step by step process. Get out of bed, shower, shave and be sure to eat something. That is what grief can do to us.

When I found myself in that kind of a "no man's land" place in life I basically had one of two choices to make, stay down and rot away or get up and live.

Our basic instinct to survive can kick in or we can kick it in and that is what I have learned. When we notice we are slipping back into a depression type state of mind it is our duty to ourselves to put a halt to the negative thinking and the lowly feelings, allow them to pass through and begin again. We can begin our life again ten times a day if we so choose to or should we actually need to. There is no written law that says we have to be an upbeat person or there are no requirements for us to participate in anything. We do it because we want to and because things around us and other people can help us to feel good. Yes, we still hurt and we still carry pain that can crop up at any given moment, we will not live in fear of it and more the opposite really, we will live in awe of the raw feelings and accept them.

Grief is something that is not totally understood in the world of psychology or anywhere. It is a love we have had for the person who has died. A respect we carried with us for a person all of our life and then they were no longer there for us to express our love to or for us not to be able to show respect to anymore. We are left holding the bag, the bag of feelings that we are supposed to be directing at them, but they are not there to receive it. We are left with all these feelings inside of us for a person who is no longer there. We begin to feel down because we have nowhere to direct those feelings, just an empty open space where we think there should be someone. I am a man and I have lost my two sons and I have no sons to direct my love to. How sad is that? It is totally fine though; I carry them with me in other ways and the effort I put into my books and my wiring is because they have died.

I write for you to maybe help piece some things together for your life because I have walked a long path figuring out stuff in mine. This is where I can direct my love for my sons. This helps with grief.

Dreaming Big

Dreams are a wonderful thing; I have no degree in the matter, nor do I claim to know how our dreams come about. I have heard that dreams are a compilation of imagination and reflections of real things that have happened. We can sometimes dream of a better life, like winning the lotto and owning our own island or something. We can dream of love and wish for things to happen in our life just as they would in a soppy love story movie, fairytale kind of. There are tons and tons of dreams that can occur in our life and we can be quite happy to wake up from an awesome dream. Do we dream as a way to fool ourselves? Is it the perfect form of delusion? Do we dream so as to escape from something else around us that we are not happy about?

I can recall daydreaming when I was about 8 years of age in school. Something used to happen in the afternoons when the sun was shining through the windows. Heat on my sweater and the classroom air seemed like almost dead really. I can recall always drifting off on those times of the day. I cannot recall exactly where I would drift off to, but I do remember even being caught by a teacher and asked a question on the most recent piece of whatever they were teaching at that time. This suggests to me that there is a little escape mechanism perhaps that is brought about by daydreaming. The boredom of school in the afternoon and a little daydream occurred, I was probably winning a trophy for a soccer match. My little mind as a child perhaps didn't have big extensive type dreams at only 8. What can your dreams do for you? Where do you bring yourself to when you dream? What kind of life do you see yourself in and or where do you end up in the dreams? I ask you so that you can ask yourself.

Dream big is what I have always told myself and to dream big could mean so many different things to so many different people, this is why it is important that we focus on you now again. Where do you go? If we aim high and "shoot for the stars" it is not about reaching the stars and ending up in isolation all alone at the top of the top. If we aim high and we do not make it all the way, there is a very good chance you have reached much higher than you ever really expected and definitely a new height way far above where any would have expected of you. Though you might not have reached the stars you will have reached somewhere far higher by making the attempt to go as high as possible.

I always believed in keeping one step ahead, ahh no not one step ahead of the rest, one step ahead of the fellow in front of you. This is a concept worth pausing on for a moment. One step in front of the fellow ahead of you. Dreams can become reality and we can live a life where we morph into the dreams, we have laid out for ourselves. It is not just a lucky few who can achieve great heights in life, no, this is a place that is reserved for us all. If you wish to be a success in your own life, all you have to do is have that dream and it can come true.

There is nothing stopping anybody from being famous or successful, nothing at all. The idea of having the dream is to create how it will all look. When you can see your dream and have a vision of how you will become and what you will be like, then it is possible to get on track and meet that dream. If you wish to succeed in your life and at whatever stage in your life this may be, then it is totally possible. Ya see we can make our dreams come true. Not in the sense of winning the lottery, but something like that is not outside the realm of possibility either.

I have also heard it said that dreams can often have metaphors of all kinds show up and some people make a living out of dissecting people's dreams and explaining them back to us. They dissect the metaphors and analyze the meanings and help people figure out what might be going on in their life. Our feelings can lead us into dream is what I believe. Sometimes when we are anxious or on edge about a day approaching in our week ahead, we might have a dream at night where we wake suddenly from our sleep.

A dream for example, we are being chased by somebody weird in a car, we are walking along a country roadside and then we feel a car driving really slowly behind us. We begin walking faster and try to look back slightly, but we cannot see a face in the car. As we walk faster the car is speeding up to keep up with us, we begin to jog. As we are in our dream, we do not even have a clue that it is a dream. Our mind keeps us running and the car is still following us. As we reach the corner in the road, we turn down an alleyway. Funny thing is we started the dream along a road where there were no buildings but all of a sudden, we are in an alleyway. We come to the end of the alley and there is a fence. The car is entering the alleyway and we must jump the fence, it is the only way. They are getting closer in the car. The car lights are lighting up the fence now as the car is approaching closer and closer. The 6 to 8-foot-high fence is easy for us to scale and get over but we are in a panic now and we jump on the fence to climb it. We fail on the first attempt. We take a three-step run this time and as we hit the fence and grab the top, we can hear the car come to a stop right behind us. The car door opens as we scramble up to the top. We are throwing one leg over the fence as we have now made it and we hear the car door slam shut. We know in our panic that they are jumping out to grab us and as we draw up our trailing remaining leg, we feel a hand grabbing for our ankle.

This is the bit where we wake up. We have no idea what just happened, did we make it, or did they grab a hold of us? We are breathing a little faster than normal and it is a very still quiet night. Nothing is going on in our bedroom. There are no car lights or people grabbing for our ankles. Just us in our sleep. By the almighty powers of suggestion, you may end up having this dream someday, apologies for planting the seed. But what can the dream mean? Sometimes it is only one piece of the dream that is or can be important, for example the dream about someone following us could be the key piece and they are driving slowly behind us, watching. This could be because we have a sneaky suspicion that someone is always watching us in our work. We feel that there is someone in our office trying to keep an eye on us just so as they can perhaps out do us if a promotion should open up. We never see a face because we have not got a clue who it might be. Then again that could have been created out of paranoia. Perhaps it is the entering the alleyway and why did our dream put an alleyway in there? That would suggest to me that our mind knew we were going to a dead end and there would be a fence, so the end of the dream was already set before the alleyway even appeared in our dream. But how can we have already set the ending if it hasn't occurred yet? Our mind knew that we needed a dead end. Maybe in our life we are feeling a little dead-end like that particular week, this could be the significant part of the dream and we are anxious inside because of a feeling of being in a dead-end situation. We are facing something in our emotional self this particular week and we must overcome it as it is holding us back. What could this be? It is not a person as we do not see any other person in our dream. The fence is representing this obstacle to us and our "must do" piece of the dream is to overcome the obstacle.

Our dream has even created a fear/panic theme to it and so perhaps it is possible that we fear overcoming the obstacle in front of us. We had to make a second attempt at getting over the fence also could be the significant piece in our dream, this may mean we have almost given up on one of our goals and our dream is letting us know we need to make another attempt in order to clear the obstacle.

I mean, I don't really know to be honest these are just some of the ideas of how our mind is working all of the time with dreams and helping us by showing us a way through whatever it is we need help with. In our dreams like this it is like our mind knows the future already. Our dream is telling us to make the second attempt. In our dream we are beginning to panic and our fears are not stopping us, we do achieve to scale the fence and we are atop the fence and have one leg already over it and as we pull the other one up, there is somebody grappling at our ankle. Is this the significant piece that our mind is telling us that we can achieve it and somebody or anybody will try and hold us back, we must make the second attempt to achieve it and our fear cannot stop us. How did our mind manufacture the scenario and how did our mind know how to set it all up? Setting things up to show us a way forward perhaps. Again, this would suggest our mind and remembering that our mind is a culmination of all of our senses and feelings along with our thoughts and our brain, so how did the mind know what is to come ahead? Can we predict the future or better yet, do we see it?

These ideas are all only possibilities, our dreams can be made up of our feelings and whatever is going in our lives. So, what piece of our dreams actually know the future? Maybe none of it as the point at which we woke up is when we were almost caught but almost to the next street, clear of any danger. We never saw the future piece of it, nor did we ever see the person grabbing for us. So, we didn't see a future in the dream, so perhaps we know nothing of the future either.

Where does the phrase "self-fulfilling prophecy" come from? What does it mean? As a layman and this being my written work to suggest that it is possible to have a handbook for life, is this a self-fulfilling prophecy of my own. I planted a seed inside of myself to write a book that others can use to discuss with self about life and take notes and try techniques to calm oneself and begin again in life or in any given day. Using relaxation as a tool and breathing as a tool to overcome all and any obstacles. It is indeed what I believe in and has been proven true to myself, so I decided to share with you, hence the title "Layman's Handbook in Life". I have a vision for this and I see this in my dreams, I see how people will buy this book and it will help them work through situations in their lives. I see people who do not normally even read, pick up this book and read pieces now and again and as they try some of what I have suggested and then they will read even more, because of course the simple things I am suggesting do actually work. This is why I have said many times, do not just take my word for it. Be argumentative and go ahead and try some of the breathing and the relaxation, see how it can be. I have never been so confident of things that can work, and this is why I have the vision of what I see. Is this a dream or is this just me creating a "self-fulfilling prophecy?

If we can see our dream and if our dream already knows parts that are in the future, then it only makes sense for us to dream big. We can take a little control over where we set our sights and really go for it. By the way it is July 2019 right now and I am writing this book, well this section anyway, it will be interesting at what time are you reading this and this will give an idea as to how far my dream has gone and what date it is now. A great thing would be that if you were to write a review for this book you include in the review, "I read this book on date __/__/____." this can become something all who do read here will know about but only after they have gotten this far and understand why you have left your review the way in which you did. I guess a wink wink emoji would be good here.

Back to dreaming big though. It is my firm belief that we can precondition ourselves into whatever we want to become. We can fix our mind on a goal and we can begin by telling ourselves about how it will be. We can envision our successes; we have the ability to set our goal in place and we can see where we will be in say 5 years. We can set our goals and fix our dreams to where we will be in 5 months. We can also set any time frame for ourselves and if we are having a bad day we can adjust and set our sights to 5 hours from now or even

5 minutes. So, given that we can do these things by actively and consciously planning them, then we can dream big and achieve big. It is possible that if we feel our way into how we can achieve things then it becomes easier to achieve them. It will not serve us any good purpose to condemn ourselves from the very get go. It is important to achieving our dreams that we allow our self to focus with a positive outlook towards our goals. To date in my own life I have not gotten too much help from others where anyone gave me a handout or any kind of free lunch. Anything I have achieved has been down to my own determination and the setting my mind to a task or a project or to keep in line with this chapter, when I have set my mind to achieve my dream it has happened.

Looking back over these things was not a clear and set out way in which I have lived my life, or it has not been some conscious decision I made when I was 5 years of age or anything. I always have had the determination and when I set my mind to something, I achieved it. Some more examples if you care to entertain them with me. Basically, I want to kind of outline to you how I have had some dreams and I achieved them. It was of course only in reflections after losing my two sons that I took some time to take stock and begin to see life and all that has gone before me of how I have managed to be where I am and who I am. Something about the loss of my children changed the lenses in which I view things in life. I began to see in a much clearer way.

When I was a child in school, I was considered to be a high achiever, why? Because I got good grades and nothing seemed to phase me in so far as academically. I set my mind to whatever lessons there were and I just did them. I had no goal or any of that kind of stuff for school and I actually dropped out of school at a very young age. For those of you reading this little bit of info who have completed all schooling, I can only say, I do not know entirely what life has been like for you. I have no idea what it was like to have, A prom night or what it was like at 16 when school and feelings and life were difficult. I can remember though how when I was a kid in school at 7 and 8 years of age that school didn't excite me too much. I did at those times though have dreams about winning soccer trophies. I wanted to win a cup for sports, I do remember explicitly wanting to have more trophies and medals for sports. We collectively were a group of little children who went out and won our league and some trophies. This was a dream of mine and every Sunday when we went to play, each day was part of the overall dream/plan. It is like even back then I knew it was going to happen. It meant each and every Tuesday and Thursday we must train to become better and eventually we will win & we did WIN.

I also as a young guy went to swimming lessons with a swimming club. Each year they had swimming races and I won those too. I wanted to win them, I saw that I needed to practice, and I went on to win. These would be very much the times where the seed had been planted in my head that if I want to win something then I better see me winning and practice like hell to get there.

When my father passed away much later in my life although, I was still young and only 29 at the time of his passing, I wanted to have a job where my father would be proud of me. My father was an architect and my entire life as a child, everything was explained to me by him using a pen and paper to draw things out. He was an architect through and through alright. I wanted to show my dad I could be something and after his death in a way to show him (which I might add, I was unaware of at the time) that I could do the things he had thought me. I began a small construction type company and then all of a sudden one day I was in a meeting with some architects and engineers. This was a bidding meeting for a new job and with my colleague at the time the plans were all laid out for the job. I took to them like a fish to water as I had been seeing architect plans my entire life. I drove home from that meeting that day with a massive sense of achievement and a feeling of how proud I was, that my dad would be so proud of me with my measuring tapes and my knowledge on how to read plans. I didn't study any of this stuff it all had been planted early in life by my father and not even intentionally.

When I did drop out of school, I did not have some laid out plan of what to do or how I was going to do it. Actually, I went a long roundabout way in my teenage years. How and ever I was a commercial fisherman in Skerries, Dublin,

Ireland. This is what I did. While I was fishing and through those years, I branched out a little bit and fished a little more around other ports in Ireland, I wanted to fish everywhere in the world. I thought that because I didn't have a formal education and no college or degrees in any subject or career type life, the only way to succeed in the field in which I had chosen was to fish around the world. I didn't need a formal education as I had my work experience and I was putting my time in to fish and this could be done anywhere there is a sea in the world. I was about 16 at that time and some few years later I found myself fishing in the Bering sea in Alaska and on down through the Pacific Ocean too. I had now fished and been in waters around the world from the little seaside town of Skerries in Ireland to Dutch harbour Alaska, Puget sound in Seattle, bend Oregon and San Francisco, California. That being the Pacific Ocean. I went from having a dream about such a thing as travelling to work on fishing boats and I did it just like how I had a goal to work in an arena that would make my dad proud, I achieved that too.

Enough about me though, I wanted to just highlight some of these things to let you know how if we have a dream and we are willing to see it through with hard work and stay focused then it can indeed come true. This is why it is always important to dream big. I like to think of a simple strategy to work off is to set short term goals, goals that are achievable. Little things, like for me they could be how I am going to maintain the lawn or garden area for the summer. This is something I can achieve and is not a massive life changing goal or anything. It is a goal I can achieve and so when I cut the grass each time and when finished I can look back and know with pride, I am achieving my goals. So, for this concept I suggest to you to have short term achievable goals. Little things that you can do weekly and when you begin to feel how good it is to hit your targets then you can begin to see out the bigger stuff too. Ya see the feeling is wonderful and it is easy to build on when we stay realistic about what we wish to achieve. It is from meeting the little ones that the bigger ones just become smaller too. Each time we reach a goal in our lives it just simply raises the bar a little each time and so our little goals become bigger and we begin to achieve them more easily as we become a machine for accomplishing anything, we set our minds to. It is by setting out in our mind that we will do it and that nothing can stop us is what will help you get there.

When I see that my first ever book TWO sons TOO many has been sold in over 14 different countries and received in excess of 40, 5-star reviews. It is this that shows me how hard work and setting goals can be achieved. Never mind the fishing around the world or sitting in an IRS audit because my little company had done almost 2 million dollars in projects.

The small things count very much in helping ready yourself for taking down the bigger goals. It is in keeping our dreams alive and fueled that we can achieve them. Some of our friends from time to time will make attempts to knock our dreams and even create a little self-doubt inside of us. If we wish to listen to the nay-sayers and if we wish to entertain self-doubt, then perhaps it would be best not to even have dreams. Why set ourselves up to fail? This is a good word "fail". I see no place for even using this word, but I am aware that some of you might actually be struggling to get your dreaming and achieving off the ground. Another belief of mine is that it is all about how we shape our dream and what words we allow into our mind that can shape how we perform in succeeding. Self-doubt has no place, even though it is natural, I understand that it can be something to struggle with, I sincerely request of you to stamp it out and maintain focus on dreaming big.

It is your own duty to yourself as a human being to set your targets, stick to them and focus on achieving your smaller goals. This is a pattern for success that you will easily move on to tackling and achieving your big dreams.

STAY FOCUSED

Loving Myself

In today's world we all seek some sort of approval or other from others. What on earth is that about and where did it slip into society? There has always been in Ireland this stupid idea or concept of "oh my god what will the neighbours think?" let's just begin with,

who on earth gives a fuck what the neighbours think!

With that now off my chest, perhaps we take a look at why we are or have become so obsessed with what other people think of us. I ask you a couple of simple questions about people around you and what on earth they do for you to bring about or give cause to extend in your own mind some little time for what others think about you. I do of course understand, and we can see all around us with social media that the world has taken to these tools as the single most common use of the Internet ever. Everyone posting updates and statuses and what lovely holiday pictures and birthday pictures. It is hard to keep up with it all. The pressures are on and they do not stop either. Back in the days of before the Internet and the instabooktwitsnap, there was a saying of "keeping up with the Jones'". The idea being and the joke of it is that if the Jones family across the street or down the road got new curtains or blinds for their windows then it is was upon you to make sure and run to the blinds shop (drapery) and get your curtains updated as well. It became a joke of when people were kind of trying to outdo each other and have something a little newer and a little better and so the arms race of the suburbs was in full flight, well not arms race really but same kind of idea. Just as the United States wants better war heads and missiles than Russia, so goes the way that keeping up with Jones went. Now we have the Internet and I like that title for social media of "instabooktwitsnap" it is not only possible to know what the Jones family are doing and how well they are doing it, everyone is at it. Updating and showing off how wonderful life is. This can be how we can understand what pressures might be on any individual in society today.

If we were to remove some of these tools of social media, we might live a little bit more relaxed in our lives. We may also find that there is no actual need for any of it and we could have more minutes in our days to focus on ourselves and not others. I know, I know, right about now you are saying that you do not spend much time on these things and that it is others who are obsessed with the Internet that have a problem with it. Good question, how long before we have to see therapy clinics for Internet use? It is not just those who spend all day every day on the Internet that may be in trouble or vulnerable to the browsing. Once upon a time there was nothing to browse per hour of each day. You didn't know how someone's holiday was until they invited you over to look through the photographs they had taken, this often happened some months after their return as it took them a few weeks to send the roll of film in to be developed in to photographs and then it took a week for that and by the time they got them and got around to inviting you over, usually by then their sun tan from their holiday had already faded. Now we can know within seconds of the person taking the snap where they are and what they are wearing and drinking or eating. If you can tell me that this is not absolutely absurd then I don't know what is. How and ever what has any of this got to do with loving myself?

What do others do for us? What can other humans be able to show us by posting all their photographs to help us understand ourselves? There is one definite and that is that by seeing all of other people's updates and statuses that we can pressure ourselves into having to take part and so we, not totally intentionally, we will take part by finding our own stuff to share with others too. By participating in this, well it obviously works because the whole world is at it. So, by participating and then somewhere on down the food chain is a person maybe a little less fortunate that does not have the luxurious holidays to flaunt around to everybody or the new car or whatever it may be. Some people don't even have nice food plates to snap and share with the world. What if the person that is less fortunate is me or you? How can we compete or take part in the updates? What does it do to our own self-esteem and how do we compensate for this?

Loving myself is about more simple things, one hour browsing the Internet and updated friends posts on social media in a day is one hour we could have spent loving ourselves. 1 whole hour per day where we focused on just us. It would be nice to think that we have the time to just allow ourselves to be with ourselves and hear our own thoughts, a part of our day where we can reflect on our Polaroids in our mind. Our reflections of the memories we have created in our life. Instead of browsing the Internet and seeing what everyone else had for dinner last night, perhaps we can reflect on the lovely meal we had ourselves. We could even take a half of an hour in our day to prepare another beautiful meal and enjoy it with our loved ones, creating yet again another pure and sweet memory for our lives.

Enriching our own life can be hard to do sometimes and finding the time can be difficult although we see nothing wrong with some social media browsing in our day, time we could have spent on our own life. One simple key factor I have always understood was that if when we bring our head to the pillow at night to sleep, can we fall asleep easily? This is something that matters to me. It is important that my mind can be clear and only to focus on my sleep is important, what is it that others on the Internet can do to help me sleep at night? What is there in the world that will help me rest my head at the end of my day and as I lay down that I will have a feeling of contentment with myself? These are a couple of questions I suggest we all ask ourselves and see what piece of being online and cruising around the internet can do to help me find this beautiful thing called "peace".

It is with a number of years of experience in searching for this peace that I have found myself actually loving myself. When I realized there was not much else that actually mattered other than being able to rest and relax when it actually came to the end of my day. This peace that forms inside one's self is not something found on any internet nor anywhere in competing in the game of life. Peace, can you have peace in life when your mind is working too hard? This brings me to the understanding of what life can mean and what is important in loving myself.

Many will say or most probably think that loving yourself means buying yourself nice new things or being super selfish with money and only spoiling yourself. There are ideas that it means taking three or four sun holidays a year and blasting them all over the Internet for people to see and maybe even be jealous of you. Yes, it is very nice to have nice clothes and comfortable clothes at that. It is also nice to go to a spa and receive a massage every now and again and it is indeed wonderful to go out to restaurants and be served beautiful meals every evening if you like. All these things are beautiful.

Peace, where does peace in our lives come from though? Eating out and having a belly full of food is a satisfying feeling for a temporary time. A comfortable feeling of being full, not bad and rewarding sometimes to sit and have a somebody wait on us. Does it bring about any peace though? Please do not get me wrong, I am not saying one must live like a hermit or something and never get out and enjoy some fine dining, nor would I ever suggest that you neglect yourself or punish yourself into not enjoying some of the nice things that are out there in life. Many people will say they are on that quest for happiness, "in pursuit of happiness" is a big part of their journey. I am saying however, if we can change some of the words around and begin to see that in the pursuit of peace may well be a better form of a saying to be part of the quest in life.

Going back to having people around us or involved in our life is a big piece of how we will rest our head at night. We may have a family and knowing all are okay can leave us at peace each evening. Being able to rest our head on our pillow at night knowing we have had a good fulfilling day and all obstacles of that day have been overcome and having been in touch with how we feel is the best way to accomplish an inner peace that will reward us so much that we will almost all of the time fall deeply & madly (in love with ourselves) asleep. This peace is priceless.

How can we accomplish such a peaceful state? What does be at peace or with peace actually mean?

One can be a person of high pace and a steady type lifestyle, someone who needs stimulation all of the time and to slow down our life would just be like saying we should not do what we do, or we cannot be who we are. No matter how fast paced you are, you can always slow down for some "me time". Me time is loving myself yes and again it really needs no introduction. Relaxations and some breathing are all we need to bring about a balance to our feelings and our thoughts, for them to come into line with each other is a way in which we can find peace. No rambling thoughts in our head and no unsettled issues to cause our feelings to be bringing about any hurt or pains. Acceptance of who we are along with an understanding of how we think, these are how I find peace. Knowing there is no yard stick created by society that I must live to and there are no Internet posts that I must compete or keep up with can allow us to have all the "me time" we need. An acceptance of how our life is going along exactly how it is supposed to be is a hard thing to find not only on the surface but inside of our entire being. There might even be something a tad unusual about us if there is nothing that anybody else has that we do not want, we can begin however with being at ease with all we have in our life and all that is around us. A great place to practice peace is in nature. Nature is all around us and if we take a moment to admire a flower and see how the flower is strong in its own right, stands firm even as it sways in a wind, the bright colours are easily visible and make up for much of the beauty of a meadow. The flower is not in competition with any other flower in the same meadow, however it is reaching for the same sunshine just like all the other flowers. The flower will provide for the birds and the bees with its beauty and is there to be appreciated and admired by all.

I do suggest taking some time in a meadow or a park and see if you can find a little flower and sit with it. Enjoy how it looks and how it's colours are just so, natural. Enjoy how it might sway in the wind or breeze which can show us how we can live and instead of trying to stand hard against a wind, it sways. The mighty oak tree again comes to mind, if you can find a tree, a mighty oak or a redwood even, oh how impressive are redwoods, wow. The tree again mighty and stood firm in the ground, helping our planet breathe, providing nuts and berries for all kinds of wildlife. When the storm hits, the tree begins to sway also. If the mighty tree were to dig in and fight back against the wind it may very well crack and break, so it sways to the wind, the branches swinging away in a storm. What can these items in nature show us about our life? That we are meant to be and are an important part of the world around us, that when the winds come and the storm begins to pick up strength in its wind, yes that's right they sway. If we can sway and bend in life, we may very well have a great chance at not cracking or being snapped. The tree almost dances in the wind and so when we feel a breeze coming perhaps some movement of our body can helps us to feel calmer as all hell is breaking loose around us. There is peace in nature to be enjoyed and to become part of it is all about getting out in it and enjoying it to the full that we can. Allowing ourselves to feel alive within nature is a beautiful place to be. Appreciating everything our planet has to offer us and allowing ourselves to feel. It is these feeling parts of us that make us unique, embrace being unique and accept who you are. No matter if you are a great big oak or a slender pine tree, you have a valuable role and part to play in life. Look at how the very prickly thorn bush of the rose is so sharp and can cut yet has such a pretty flower. All things have their reasoning and finding your own piece of how you are and who you are, are what can bring you to a place of peace in your daily living. Allowing yourself to feel, yup the feelings are oh so important about being at peace. Accepting the way life is, is a beautiful way to find a path to peace also. Loving myself is a wonderful path to peace.

Peace is a great reward and probably the single greatest reward for loving myself. Peace is a place where I can enjoy everything around me from a simple sip on my tea to the feel of sun on my face. I am not in need of the Internet or people to enjoy this place of peace.

The haters are always going to hate, and so do I need such people? The people who wish to keep me down and or are not supportive in my shooting for the stars, do I need them to take away from my peace? I know you can answer that quite easily.

Peace is a place that is sacred to you and your life. Enjoy it and always allow yourself to feel when you are there, it is the balance of our feelings that helps us achieve such peace in the first place. The distractions we have allowed to halfway take over our life and the rat race we compete in daily do not have a place in our peace. This is what I call loving myself and with just these few tidbits, I do of course hope you can begin to love yourself and gain a peaceful time in each of your days in life. There are no Internet posts that are going to create this kind of peace for me. It has come about for me by allowing myself to feel. When I am at one with my feelings, I feel a great sense of balance. My mind works to a point of sometimes I am in awe and absolutely amazed at how clear life has become.

How do I achieve this? I relax and I meditate in the world around me. I do my breathing exercises outside in nature and allow the beauty of the world be part of my life.

These are the real techniques that I hope you try from time to time. It has not been from the internet nor is it that I have said to you to do this. It is my sharing of my little secret and you doing it. You doing it is the part that will let you have a smile from ear to ear and you will not thank me for it. It is yourself you will thank for actually allowing yourself to take the time and breathe in nature.

This is pure, happy, Peace. This is loving myself. Repeat the words.

DIRECTIONS

I went to a comedy show not too long ago and the comedian who was telling us all kinds of funny laughable stuff, he took a moment to explain to some non-Irish people in the audience of how Irish people are. He wanted to point out how we the Irish always ask questions. We do not give up any information at all when asked a question but more like we just add another question as an answer, I wish to give him his rightful credit as he was very funny indeed. I will look him up and let you guys know who he is. His point was that on his way to the show that evening as it was in the city of Dublin and he was not from the city he would have to ask somebody the way to the comedy club. "hey, excuse me I am a little lost, can you tell me which way it is to the comedy club?" the emphasis was on how he would ask an Irish person and the response would be, "well which direction would you be coming from?" he mentioned how he could continue down the street and stop another and ask, "hey I am not from the city, could you tell me how to get to the comedy club" & the response from the Irish person would be "would you be walking or driving?". And so on went the skit, the laughable thing about it was how he was pointing out something that is very true about Irish people and how they will immediately respond with a question. Sometimes they are already thinking of their question before they have fully heard what you are saying. This can happen in a ton of cultures and is not exclusive to the Irish at all.

As an Irish person I implore you to have as many questions as possible, why? It is from asking questions that new questions are born and so on goes the cycle. By having questions, we stand a chance of learning something, if we are learning anything we are growing, and this makes for a great way to exercise our mind and bring new things into our life which can be enriching for us. The comedian was pointing out about the tons of questions we have in response to questions and he was simply asking for directions. What do we do when we are lost? We ask for directions. This would be the simplest answer to an actual event of being physically lost in a location. In a new city perhaps or on road trip to where we know the destination, but we are unsure how to get there, these are being physically lost and we ask for directions. Now how about you find yourself a little lost in your own life, your own feelings are a bit of a mystery to you and it is difficult to find your way. This is about you as a person physically but is not the same as being lost in a city. Finding your way in a city can be as mundane as a few turn lefts and turn rights, what on earth or how can this compare to the mystery of being lost inside of ourselves?

This is something that is not new to us humans and being Irish we have many tourists who come to our country on a "sabbatical" and quite often they will tell us of how they "are trying to find themselves". An older man from a rural part of Ireland had told me one time that he encounters many such tourists. He explained to me that he could not figure out why they all come to Ireland to be lost. He saw no sense in this and he continued to explain to me that he had one simple answer for all who he encountered that were of the same frame of mind. He stands square in front of them and places a hand on each of their shoulders and looks them straight in the eye and tells them " you say you are trying to find yourself? I can now tell you that you are right here in front of me. You are found, now off home with you". That is his simple concept, and nothing makes any more sense really. Another great concept of directions and lost is how the saying of "not all who wander are lost", what can that mean to us if we are feeling lost, are we really lost?

What is it about a sense of direction that we can find ourselves bogged down in an idea that we have no direction? No matter how we feel, we are definitely heading somewhere, do we need to know all of the time? What direction is your life going right now? I am going to make a bit of a guess that you bought this book for some easy reading or it was recommended by a friend. If you happened upon it and decided to make the purchase because of a place you are at in your life, then maybe this chapter is for you especially.

To be fair and not to single you out though, we are all searching for something along our journey in life and you are not alone in this. We can in many ways convince ourselves into thinking we are feeling different things. This is done by just how it reads "thinking" there are times that feelings are foreign to us and we have our mechanisms which we have developed from birth about how we acknowledge our feelings. One of the tough ones is hurt and because we have spent many years hiding our hurt feelings, we have developed a way in which to mask it. When we hurt and another might notice and express some concern to us, we take all the tricks and power we have developed along our entire lifetime and we can often respond with "I am fine".

There are other responses to someone checking in with us that are we okay and they can fall along the lines of us responding in such ways of "it's not that I am hurt by it, I feel just so betrayed" or we can say "it doesn't upset me, I just feel like I have lost confidence" these are things that can be some very genuine responses but can also be a way in which we have developed a skill set to meander around our feelings. Another word for meander might be to say wander and that could bring us back to "lost" by word association alone.

What is it that we can begin to undo or change in how we deal with our feelings inside of ourselves? How do we change a "way" in which we have survived within for years? Do I really sometimes fake it and think I am feeling something that I am not? Or is it possible that I just never actually knew what this particular feeling was, so I just labelled it myself because of what I thought it was meant to be called? If that doesn't get you lost in a hurry then nothing will, lol. There are two very distinct things going on inside of us as we continue on our life path.

1 of which is how we think, what we say when we are thinking about something.

The second is of how we feel. They are quite different and one does not control the other in any way at all.

How we allow one to overpower or take precedent is in our own choosing. If I am to ask you right this very second, how are you feeling? Pause............................ (write here, what you feel)

What might the answer be? Should an answer to this question begin with, "I think I feel okay" for example. Or perhaps, " I think I am alright now". I could ask another question of you for right now and this would be "how do you feel about the direction of your life?" pause..
(write down your answer)

If you find the answer to be "I feel quite good about it", or "I feel like I could be doing better". These are examples of the difference between how we think and what we feel. Quite often we can begin an answer to these questions with the think and feel pieces a bit muddled up. If someone were to ask you what do you think about something, then naturally the response would begin with "I think". If someone asks you a question about how do you feel about something then the answer again would begin with the right beginning of "I feel", these are two very different points to begin with and when we have a friend who is always telling us about how they think they feel or someone that tells me this, my question is really, do they think they feel it or do they feel they think it? Confused yet?

The difference is massive, but it is a great tool we can learn from about whether we are actually aware inside of ourselves or not. We can check with ourselves and know the difference. If I were faced with a mathematical question and it required me to think about the answer, then I could say I think the answer is blah blah blah. I do not think that I have ever answered a math question by saying, I feel the answer should be blah blah blah. Do you see the difference yet?

My thoughts are deep and can sometimes go off on a completely different tangent, it is nice to have imagination and daydreaming and allow my thoughts wander off. I can create a whole scenario in my mind about anything. I might even amuse myself while I wander and create ideas and things. Sitting in the waiting room at a hospital clinic not too long ago and I found myself creating little characters out of all the people that were busy moving around. The secretaries that were behind the main desk and the nurses and doctors who would come and call each patient in turn. I was amusing myself while I was waiting, I was far enough away that I could not hear their conversations, I was creating the dialogue in my mind. I was thinking about it in my thoughts as a way to pass the time while I sat waiting, amusing myself. I did not have any great feelings attached and it was stuff I was doing with my thinking. The time did pass on mind you and then I was called.

I have heard from many people about how they hate to be in the same such waiting rooms and they think it is such a horrible experience. I did not experience any such horrible feelings sitting there waiting as I was there for an appointment and that was that. My feelings that day while there were content and happy to wait, my thoughts mind you were a little different. So I wonder if those who I have heard making complaints and saying it was a horrible experience, I wonder if they actually had feelings involved to say the experience was horrible or did they allow their thoughts to conjure up the idea of how horrible it was and did they pass the time waiting by allowing their thoughts to over crowd everything and call it all horrible. Does this mean that they actually thought themselves into believing in their own thoughts and then created an idea of a feeling surrounded by their thought? Is this possible to do?

I believe it is. If we can imagine our feelings like this, then it makes for a very confusing time indeed. Is what I am feeling right now something that is real or something I have invented throughout my life to be what I "think" it is.

Perhaps we can move in many different directions when it comes to our feelings and we can convince ourselves of feelings so strong. We can say we are in love, which is a very beautiful feeling and we can convince ourselves that we are. We can then break up with someone and then say "oh I thought I was in love with them, but now I realize what love is" so what was the love feeling you were convincing yourself of the time before that?

What is it to say "I feel so proud of somebody" does that mean when someone achieves something great it is an excuse to feel proud of them or is it that society has recommended that, that is the time and place to be proud of somebody, so we think ourselves into the idea of saying we feel proud? The world in which we live in is definitely lighting the pathway for us to proceed along the route of how we as people are supposed to feel and when to feel it. For this reason, many people out there go along with it and so convince themselves into feeling what they think they should and when they should. Now that is a tough pill to swallow even for me and it is something that I have just noticed along my own journey. It is not to challenge you or to take away from any genuine feelings you may have or ever had.

I will say that I will never forget the most genuine feeling and not because it is stated that we must "not forget", the day my first son was born was November 16th, 1996. This day will top all days as it was the day, I became a father. I could not have invented that feeling even if I tried. I was elated at the time and I probably never had felt the same thing before or since. It was my first time ever experiencing this type of thing, birth. It was a ton of so many firsts all in one moment and it was like out of this world. The feeling was something I had never felt before and was absolutely amazing. This is a feeling or a time when we are supposed to feel overjoyed and excited and to be honest overjoyed and excited are definitely understating how I felt. I had nothing to compare this feeling with as it was my first time to experience this, I could not have invented such an altogether fascinating and joyous moment even if I had tried. Almost an outer body experience really, the joy that I felt that very moment he was born became my new yard stick for feelings of immense happiness, how could anything ever even compare? Could I invent this type of feeling again or replace it or manufacture it with my thoughts? Absolutely not, there is no possible way for me to carbon copy that feeling ever. If we were face to face right now, I could probably explain how it all felt to you and by using body language and hands and expression in telling you about it, you might begin to feel like you had the feeling all by yourself. This would be how it can be that our mind can pick up on stuff and convince us to have feelings, I will definitely and always say that there is a possibility that when we think we feel a certain way then the problem is that right there we are thinking.

Feelings come from feeling and thinking comes from thought.

What would this all have to do with directions in life anyway? The path that we are on has two directions with two other directions within it, so a sub pathway if you like. We are on our journey in life and we have two certainties in our journey, one is that we definitely began our life and the journey and the other is that we will definitely come to an end in our journey. The direction that we are heading is one way and the end of our life is at the end of the path. This we can say is for sure. This is the one direction of our path, we will come to many bends and crossroads along our path and sometimes we will choose a wrong direction perhaps and though we feel it is a wrong direction or any around us see it as a wrong way, we are still constantly heading towards our end. This is one simple fact of life that you can rely on. The other direction on our path is where others may travel upon as we meet them along the way. Nobody is ever heading back towards birth so to say it is another direction on our path is to identify how others may seem like they are travelling in an opposite direction to us, but they may just be circling around to get going again. We can speed up our journey sometimes in our life and we can slow it down, this would be where the path has a kind of sub path or little piece in the center where there are alternating directions also. Sometimes we slip into there and we begin to "to and fro" back and forth and do not seem to make much progress at all. If we look at nature again there is a great way in which we can learn from the movements of the ocean. The tide comes in and the tide goes out, only ever resting for short periods of time at high water and at low water where the tide is said to be turning. If we look at our lives we can see when we fall into this little sub path area that we are either, just like the ocean, we are either coming in or going out, but we are never sitting for too long in any one position. We have all heard people speak of how they do not feel like they are heading anywhere in their life or they are lacking direction right now and they are just threading water, or they feel motionless. Look to the tide for proof, there is not much of motionless going on, the tide is always moving. The sub path where we can fall into from time to time may feel like there is not much going on but there are two very clear directions, you are either progressing on your journey or you are regressing. There is no motionless and all the while you never stop moving along the main path which is bringing you every day closer to the end.

There is a beautiful piece in a movie that can explain a lot of everything there is to know about life, the simplicity of it and the absolute facts. The movie is Castaway and the actor Tom hanks, the best piece of any movie I have ever seen to date. When the main character Tom hanks plays has been stranded on an island for a long time, for company he has Wilson which is another great piece of master writing, I believe, Tom hanks tells us all how it really is "today the sun will rise, today the sun will set" when his character acknowledges these two things he has now broken down his life into the most basic or simple version there can be, these are his guarantees from life. When we take the time to slow our own life down and see these as fact and know nothing else but these two things then we can rebuild our entire world and life.

We can set out back on our path without expectations and we can begin again knowing some very simple basic facts. Life has few guarantees and so to know these is a way in which we then can gain a great appreciation for everything else that comes across us. When we have slowed ourselves down in life to feel the sun rise and the sun set then we are for sure alive and ready for anything. Should we feel that we have become motionless and that we are stuck in the sub path of our journey then perhaps it is fair to say that we may actually be regressing in our journey, that could be in our maturity as a person or in our responsible adult way of life. Yes, we would all love to be children forever if we could, that's just not possible or practical. Our movement is just like the tide sometimes coming in and sometimes going out. So how does what we feel connect to all this?

We are always feeling every day and just like the tide the feelings, they come along and they leave. The feelings we experience will never last forever or just like in the movie castaway; the day does not go on forever. Sometimes I have heard people who are having a really bad day say "I wish this day would just end" there are times when people are having an absolutely beautiful time and they will say the opposite "oh how I wish this day would never end" sadly for one and happily for the other, the day will end just as does every day. Just like how we feel at any one time in our day or life. It does not last forever and the feelings will pass and come back again another time. Sometimes it can also be said that or at least you have heard it said before that our life is on cycles and everything goes around and round. "What goes around comes around" or the "cycle of life", again suggests something round. It can be said that as we "circle" along our path that we can run into some of the same feelings over and over again. It is possible that while we are not dealing with our feelings that they come and they go and when we circle back around again it is another opportunity to deal with them. When we finally acknowledge how we feel and deal with them by letting them out and gaining an understanding of why we feel this way or that, it is then that we have dealt with them and sometimes accepted how we feel about certain things or people, it is only then that we can progress on and the cycle can allow us continue straight for a while. I went through a full cycle of life by being at both ends of my first son's life. As I was telling you a little earlier, I was there the day he was born and then I was there the day we lowered him to his grave in his coffin. It was 15 years and 3 and half weeks apart. This was a complete cycle of life. A short life and though I missed pieces as a father, I got enough to know the absolute beauty that he was, what his life meant to me and the beauty the day he was born and the absolute sorrow the day we buried him. The feelings I have acknowledged on both occasions and the feelings I have accepted for both also. It does not take away a repeated cycle of sorrow or grief as I was saying earlier but it is part of my world now.

I do have an idea of what hurt can do to us from having such experiences as burying my children and the eye openers those experiences have brought into my life. It is the reason I am writing to you now. I am not here to give you a complete guide to life or to hold up a map and say follow this, this is the route to all salvation, nah, not even close. I am writing for you to have a read and for me to lay it out on paper to show you there are options in our lives of how to proceed. I want to suggest to you that there are things worth trying and see if you can adapt them to fit into your own life. This is not a novel and this not a memoir, this book will go in the self-help section and category to offer to you time to read and find yourself just like the old man in the West of Ireland tells everybody who asks "you are there right now where you are". There is no, oh I wish I was elsewhere or there is no I wish I was somebody else. If you ever find yourself hating your life then it is only a matter of a feeling or a thought, these can change and sometimes quickly. We can allow ourselves to stay a little stuck and we can begin a cycle of thought where we convince ourselves to remain down or in "a rut". Believe it or not we have the power to break out from the rut, we can climb out from our sub path and stop to-ing and fro-ing just like the tide coming in and going out and we can climb the mountains in life that challenge us. When we are in the mountain we can see water, the water that helps make up the tide, we can see the river at its source and we can be more like the river, one direction and the river will carve through stone and rock if it needs to as it is on its own journey. This is our life journey as we too are water. It is our decisions from our minds that can hold us back and keep us stuck or we can accept our feelings and allow our thoughts and emotions flow, just like the river. The river can be so small and a little trickle at its source and just like us as a baby vulnerable, then we grow as does the river and sometimes the river is no joke and can be ferocious and then calm again. Sometimes deep and sometimes shallow. This too can be us. The good thing about our journey in life is that we have all the options in front of us to make changes and alter our course and try new things. Just like trying on clothes, we can try something and see if it fits. We do not have to stay on our course all of the time and our path can happen to bring us many places. You will know the path you are on is right for you when you can do your relaxation and your breathing and rest your head on your pillow at night and just be.

This calm peaceful being that you can become will let you know you are on a right path. This is what I hope for you. If you are a person who has found themselves saying they hate their life, then it is for you that I ask you to consider that it is only a cycle and that you can regain your place on your path and will climb out of the sub path by slowing things down and bringing things into simple perspective. Today the sun will rise, this can be as simple as it needs be to help you gain back your traction.

Now I must ask you again.

What direction are you on in your life? (some space to scribble your thoughts if you like).

Life & Living

Some of us in the world today see ourselves living life to the max. We can turn on a TV and see extreme sports and be in awe of those who are on some cutting-edge stuff when it comes to high energy and really having a blast. Other times we go on some travel and are invited into someone else's life and we may find ourselves say or we have heard many other people say "we only thought we were living" again yes it is as it is in our society that we will compare ourselves to others and what they are doing with their lives. I can assure you that you are living too. Why do we want to compare so much anyway? Like what is it about our own life that does not feel right? I have used an example in the past about sitting in a restaurant and one couple having dinner and somewhat discussing some problems they have in their relationship and while they sit and chat about it another couple a little further away are eating in the same restaurant and they are gazing into each other's eyes and holding hands across the table while the candle makes them look like a postcard for love. One of you says as you glance across, "why we cannot be like them?". The simple reason is that you are them, they just don't discuss their problems in a restaurant and they most definitely are in love too, they like to express it differently. Just like all of us individuals in the world, we all have a different way of expression. When you think someone else is living a better life or a nicer life then the question is not about how do I live like them but more likely the better question is what is it about my own life that I am not getting the most out of?

A lot of the time this question can be answered using one word. Appreciation. Yup appreciation is a thing where we appreciate what we have, we realize that everything about our own life is exactly how it is supposed to be. Sounds easy as 1, 2, 3 doesn't it? Well it is if you think about it long enough. We all just want a little love and attention. Some may want a little more than others, this is true. Another key factor is everybody believes they are right by how they do stuff and so why then does a question of how other people are living become an issue. If everybody believes they are right about how they go about their affairs and living, then how can anybody be wrong? Of course, some of us are wrong and some of us are right, that is just like night & day existing. Everyone being right would be a bit too fairy tale. Imagine sitting in a packed restaurant and all the tables in the entire place having people in love holding hands across the table and nobody except you is doing anything other than gazing into each other's eyes. That would not only be fairy tale like, it also would be a bit embarrassing and I could nearly without any doubt say that you would probably copy everyone else and just play along so as not to be the odd one out. Again though, it is fairy tale like and just not how the world happens.

We are given life by our parents and then it is up to us how we live it. This is the beginning of our grown-up choices. I do understand that life is anything but a fairytale and that there are those of us in the world who have suffered traumatic things like abuse of many different kinds and for those who have suffered at the hands of another, I commend you for reading this far. I do not have a story about abuse, and I cannot even begin to imagine how tough and what strength it has taken you to overcome these obstacles in your journey. I am not only talking about sexual abuse but all kinds of abuse as a child and you have grown out from it and still everyday work on being a super person. Your choice to live and continue living is something to be admired and if you are a person who has suffered from abuse, let me be the first to say, well done and give yourself a pat on the back for all your hard work. You actually help tell this kind of a chapter as I wish to enter into how it is our decisions and choices on how we choose to live that can dictate to us how we do it and how we take a conscious decision not to allow any other hurtful influences make our choices for us.

As we become adults it is exactly how we choose to live that will be how we actually benefit from life and what benefits we reap and sew for ourselves. I mentioned the idea of anyone who has suffered abuse at the hands of another because they are not so fortunate to just have to make their own decisions and some have had decisions made for them. It is their decision now as an adult and just like all of us. It is our decisions that will shape how our life will be. Some of us just have had a little larger obstacle to climb and this makes the strength and power of people something to be in awe of.

Yes you, you reading right now, you are a human and you are amazing. Did you know that you are the most perfect you that you will always be? Did you stop today and tell yourself how perfect you actually are? The good old society we live in has tried to teach us from an early age that "there is no such thing as perfect", but we can try for perfection and just be accepting that it does not exist... This is so wrong it is not even funny. Something I would like you to consider for a moment or two. To me you are perfect and you are the most perfect YOU. This is something we must scratch out from our minds eye and allow ourselves to tell ourselves that there is perfection and it does exist.

When you look into the mirror every day, repeat the words. I AM PERFECT, I AM THE PERFECT ME.

Nobody else in the world is you, nobody else in the world feels like you, acts like you or thinks like you. You may find some people who have similar thoughts or have expressed some identifications with you on how they feel but you are the perfect you. So, what is so hard about living the life you want? Nothing really, just like in our dreams if you can see it then you can believe it. Haven't you always heard seeing is believing? So, what is stopping you from getting your life into focus and beginning to see it for how you want it to be?

It takes a little vision yes this is true, we touched on it in the chapter on dreams, so here we are again making the same point just a different way maybe. Perhaps I think it didn't ring through quite clearly the first time, lol. Our choices in life are to make the best life possible for ourselves, right? You do not have to compare your life to any other persons nor do you have to rely on the Internet to show you how to live. There is an exact route to everything you want in your life.

The difference with this exact route and the path or journey of your life is that you get to set the whole thing up. You get to choose who can ride with you on your journey and you get to set all the ground rules. It is a bit of work but not like having a job. There is only one boss, that is you. There are only the rules you set for yourself. What is it that you like to compare to others in life? As a woman you believe in all the beautiful models in the magazines and the airbrushing that goes on. So, you want the perfect beach body and toned and tanned and all this cosmetic type stuff. Here is an idea, begin training and set out a steady work out plan. Train hard each week and save on the side for some beach holiday to get the tan. Begin a regime of yoga and Pilates, start taking action for your own body and become responsible for it. Watch what you eat and begin taking up swimming. All of these things are designed to tone your body and help you become just like all of the women in the magazines. Now that I read back over this bit, it didn't seem that difficult of a decision, did it?

Are you a man who wants to have the muscle toned body that all the magazines also portray? It is the same kind of decisions that needs to be made. Get into the gym three times a week, work hard at toning your body and take up some yoga too. Watch what you are eating in your diet and you too can have a perfect fit and lean body. Again, this seems like an easy decision doesn't it?

Ahh but there are drawbacks to making these decisions so easily and carrying them out. We cannot commit to a regime of serious work out and we find it hard to maintain a strict diet, so what is the answer to that? Set a more achievable goal for yourself and make a decision to do what you can? This is about making a decision for your life that you will live by and then by your choice you will enjoy all the befits you can from taking control of one simple aspect of your life. That aspect, your body.

We have all seen the shows on the Internet and the TV that are called biggest loser I think one of them is called, for example. The one where people lose weight each week and hit some phenomenal targets, those shows though have trained people to help work on the person's psychology too though. They talk them through their feelings as well as having dieticians and special weight and exercise coaches. So, they have a tough though easier job because of the assistance they receive. Do you require all the same assistance? Tell yourself that either you do, or you do not need the assistance, if you do then go out and find some trainers and sign up to them. The decision on your side is to keep up the commitment. So we are talking about our physical body here at the moment, now what if we throw out some of the buzz words of today and one of them is "mental health", what if the piece of us that we wish to fine tone and get in shape is our mental health and not our physical health? What if this is the piece that we want to get in shape, can we do this just as easily? Yup why not? What is the answer as "society" has even made it like a buzz word around the whole world? What can we do with something that carries such a big stigma to it? It is just like the physical aspect of our being, we must first acknowledge that we are unhappy with the condition of it now, we must take some action to make a decision to want to bring about some change in our condition and we must move forward on following this through. Sounds too easy doesn't it? Of course, it does in theory. Let's take a quick look at what is possible. Again, just like the people training for weight loss they have people who are professionals helping them to keep up their efforts. Then in making our decision to deal with our own mental health we may just need to seek out some assistance from professionals. Oh no the stigma! What will the neighbor's think? I am attending a shrink for some help and I don't know if I am able to do it. Oh crap!

These are just little tidbits of self-doubt to hold you back. It is the barriers that we create for ourselves that are our toughest obstacles. However, they have been placed there by ourselves. If we can place obstacles in front of ourselves, then we can also remove them. It is suggested that in the safe environment of a professional therapist's office, we can begin to work on some of our issues, as sometimes tackling mental health is not as straight forward as just being in a gym. The similarities are that the gym is for training in the muscles in our physical self, the therapist's office is the gym we go to for when it is more emotional or mental fine tuning we seek. What can we do about either physical, mental or emotional conditions? We can begin by making a decision to tackle them. We can begin by breaking our life down to a simplistic place where we are in a peaceful state of meditation. We allow our feelings to come into line with our thoughts.

It is with these little tools we can accomplish not only to get a handle on ourselves but to begin to become the true champion we were born to be. Yes, yes, I hear you say, but how?

The how is in the why, why is a better question. Why do we wish to improve ourselves in any shape or form? There is nothing the matter with us could be a way of looking at it and yes of course, this is quite true. There is nothing the matter with us so the why is irrelevant and all the rest of us can just continue to go around in life to be envious of you and your all togetherness lol.

The why becomes the only reason we make any changes to our life. Why do I need to change is a great question to ask yourself? If you find 5 or 6 reasons, then the decision is probably not too far behind. If you find 9 or 10 reasons, then you probably have already tried a few times. So, what can stop you from giving up, this time? Where can you draw upon for absolute determination? The perfect you that you are deserves the very best you that YOU can give yourself. Not anybody else. Life is for living and not something that just has to be endured. When we think we have it all cracked and it does not get any better, there is always the chance it can be even nicer. A healthier you is a fantastic addition to your life.

We can plod along on our path and never be too excited about anything and go through the motions, college then job, family and home life. Sums it all up doesn't it? We can also make some decisions to not only live a life, we can decide to live the best life. We can be amazing in every aspect. Imagine that, you amazing. Yes, that is right. So, what is the formula you ask? I do not have one. You have the formula inside of yourself. Imagine that. You carry the answers and you carry the formula right there inside of yourself. Yup not me, you.

How did I learn this and why would I wish to share this with you? I can only tell you about myself and I cannot live your life for you. What I can do though is with every word I am writing now and knowing inside of myself that because of how I have adapted myself to life that I can explain or relate to you what I have learned.

What thought me about life? Was it when I was a teenager and I was abusing alcohol and drugs? Did I know when I made a decision to abide by the courts and remain in a treatment facility that I was actually improving my own mental health along with my physical self? Was I aware that life was happening to me and I was on the mend to get back on my path and stop swirling around in a terrible environment that led me to a prison cell? The answer is no I did not know any of those things at that time. It has only been in hindsight that I have learned what those times actually meant and looking back and seeing how I chose a life to abstain from drugs and alcohol was a decision I made to allow my own real self through to the world. It was not until much later in life when I realized I have been living a fabulous life and have been oh so lucky and oh so thankful for my life. Remember I mentioned the word appreciation, yup gaining an appreciation for everything life has had to offer me has brought me to a wonderful place to be able to feel my way through my day to day living. The episodes that came much later in life were of course the death of my children. When I stood by the graveside for the first time watching my son being buried (I lowered the coffin into the ground with a strap in my own hands) it was like someone reached inside of my body and ripped my heart out. I mean seriously, that is how it felt. I felt emotionally dead and my thoughts were a pure blank.

Because I had already been into living in the now, I looked up at the sky with tears in my eyes and I looked around, I was looking around to avoid any person's eye contact and I was gazing at the sky. I saw the clouds and the branches of the treetops as I stood beside an open grave where I had laid

Darra to rest. What did that take out of me? Every ounce of strength I thought I already had. And guess what, 2 years and 7 months later I was at another graveside where I was burying my second son. But this wasn't like the first one, nope this was like can I even say worse... The difference the second time round was I knew the heartache and I had nothing left to give. My heart was ripped out the first time and all the mental torture I had gone through learning about grief and what the hell is sudden death and why Darra had died. I had not even come close to coming to terms with it and then my second son Patrick had died also. I sat a deflated man in a seat beside a grave where many had gathered as with the shocking death of a baby. Darra had been 15 when he died and Patrick only 1yr and 4 months. I looked to Patrick's mom and asked her why they are not lowering him into the grave. She whispered back, they are waiting for you because you are the father, they are waiting for you to say to begin. I definitely wanted to jump in with him that's for sure. I do not recall the rest of that day too well. I do remember that night and I remember chatting with people after later on in the evening but at that graveside what was left of me felt like it died. I had just spent the last two years trying to figure out why I would cry uncontrollably at times when Darra would come to mind and now this was upon me. Patrick gone too.

Our minds can begin to get in on us when we have been faced with such horrific experiences as these traumas. Our mind, well my mind would keep asking why and what is wrong with me. Am I never to have a son who will call me dad? What is wrong with me as a human, is my seed no good? What is this bullshit thing called life and why in the hell have I had to learn about death in such a horrendous way? The negative thoughts can be explained in much more detail, but I am thinking you might be getting the picture. Where or how do I go on from here as a man? Where will I turn to rebuild myself? How can I go on living? It all seemed impossible.

This is the power of our mind and how it can convince us to give up and to stay dull and down. We can invent a smile just as easily as we can sit silently in a chair and not speak for hours. What I couldn't control in my time immediately after Patrick's death were the tears. The tears are the hardest thing and when they came, they would come hard and with an actual physical pain inside of my gut. This physical pain was like a sharp pain with an unmerciful thud, like a direct blow from a boxer with a sharpness to the end of the blow. I had not got a clue sometimes if it was day or night. There were times I could not tell you if I had eaten or not and there were times that I thought I was going absolutely stir crazy.

These are some of the reasons that I can testify to how we have some choices in our lives as to how we comprehend what is going on around us and what might be needed to do to get ourselves back on the horse in life. We become faced with decisions. I could perhaps sit and wallow and starve myself to death or I could continue in the world as a normal looking person with an absolute mountain of hurt inside. Something happened to me as a person and the way in which I viewed everything. I had already become a person who believed in feeling his way through life and enjoying and savoring most of the beauty around me. These kinds of feelings, living and in the now habits I had developed back when I was 17 and giving up on drugs and alcohol. Now all of a sudden it didn't seem so beautiful anymore. Where will I find the strength to continue and grow out from this. How will I manage to stay straight with my emotional turmoil and the thoughts that keep racing through my mind? I like anyone who may endure some emotional or mental problems now was someone who didn't carry a sign above my head that said, "I have lost my children and am hurt, please go easy on me". I do not carry one of those signs by the way lol.

It did not make for an easy time let me assure you of that. What it did though was make me reflect on my entire life. I looked over all kinds of issues and I began to see things differently. I saw how we do have choices in the most bizarre of situations and I learned that there is no other power outside of ourselves that can make us or break us. As humans we are fragile and with a world of hurt and mental torture to endure there is no escape to any better place than to just begin to deal with it.

Life and living is waiting for us all. To live in this world, I have found that when we can break it all down to some basic foundations, the fundamentals of life. What do we need? It is nice to be loved by another yes, this is true but what do we need? What are our basic needs? Water is a basic need and some nourishment. We need air that we breathe, and this was enough for the beginning, what else can we do after that?

We must breathe the air that is all around us and this is why I harp on about taking the time to do some breathing exercises. I also found that in order to be able to perform in any kind of way in life we must be able to have rest, our sleep is important to us. How can I sleep if I have not got peace in my brain? This is why the breathing and meditating are such a huge part of helping us make the changes we may need in our life. The meditation can allow our feelings to come through. When our feelings pour out from us and are done so in a relaxed way where our concentration is on our breathing, we can sit and cry and smile and all kinds of things which in turn then will allow us to bring a calm and a peace to our mind. This is the key to getting our sleep. With sleep we can function and we can begin each new day anew. Yes of course I am still a grieving father, but I have made the conscious decisions to live life and continue. I am set to enjoy all of it. There is nothing than can knock me as I have had to rebuild myself in life a few times and very much from the ground up again and again. Why do I encourage you to try stripping away some of the society bull crap that you have been listening to for years? Because quite simply it is the way in which I have found to be able to live. Remember how I had mentioned in the beginning it is that we are given the gift of life when we are born. Well it is our decisions and choice that can determine how we live. When we make conscious decisions and put the work in, just like going to the gym, it is then that we can start living no matter the excuses we have formulated inside of our heads. Life and living are very precious and when we gain an appreciation for them it is then that all else will calm and allow us to focus on our work on self. There is not some formula that I say works for me and gives a reason for you to be in awe of me, absolutely not.

You can take as an example what I have had to learn and come through to adapt into your own life some of the techniques and begin to overcome your own obstacles. It is the work you will put into yourself that I fully hope is going to leave you in awe of you.

Please write 5 points of commitment to yourself here below as a starting point.

1.

2.

3.

4.

5.

Word to the Wise

Man! There are so many gurus out there these days that have some very powerful messages and it is here that I will actually agree with the Internet having a great power by being able to reach all over the world in only a matter of a few minutes. Something can begin trending in like seconds and then be absolutely viral within the first few minutes. This is so cool that some of the great messages can reach as many people as possible in such a short space of time. If you are aware of some of these great things, then you do know how all the positivity that is shared can be just the right tonic for your day sometimes. I often even share some of my own thoughts through a blog that I write and at different times I will make a post on one or other of the social media sites. There is nothing nicer than receiving feedback from people to hear it was something they "needed to hear today" or sometimes I get a simple "thanks for sharing". It is these things that help me continue on doing such posts of videos or blogs and even some of the poems I write. It is when someone actually goes out of their way to acknowledge that my own work and my own thoughts are appreciated by another. The better feeling is that somebody out there actually understands and has shown me by their way of expressing a "thank you". There are a number of reasons that I have taken to writing and to sharing stuff all over the Internet with you and the main one as you can tell, well there are two of them. My sons and in their dying have inspired me to share my story and share my learning from these experiences. My experiences are of course of an entire lifetime, but their passing was something that spurred me on to look back over it all. I am out there and probably the reason you have found me here or somebody else has done a Retweet or a further share of one of my posts and it has caught your eye. I am very glad you found me, and I have found you.

So, the abundance of positivity that is shared around the Internet is wonderful and when you are feeling down or not too into positivity it is almost like unavoidable which can in turn add to your downward spiral. When viewing the world on any given day through some lenses of not such a great viewpoint let's say, the more we bump into "positivity" we can find it a little hard to escape from it and this does make it harder. Some days we need to have an off day and just wallow in whatever form of self-pity we have conjured up that day. There is nothing amiss with allowing oneself to stoop down a little from time to time and it can also help propel us to our next great new high. The sayings are numerous and like the archer who in order to hit his target must pull back on his bow and arrow first. This way he can then release it and the arrow is shot hard to hit the bullseye. Our lives can be quite similar and if we stop to look at some of it, then yes perhaps we too do need the little pull back before we head to our next target.

Just very much like who controls the world of money, we can look at the stock market on wall street. The markets will make a correction to themselves and stocks will begin to plummet one day, the markets will close, and it will be called a "down day". History and all the financial people can read the trend and see the down day and realize it is simply a market correction and things will return to somewhat normal stability. These are everyday signs of life happening around us and it is okay to allow ourselves to take some time when we do not feel totally up to it.

What are the wise words or words to the wise though? When we find ourselves surrounded by absolute positivity it can be just as damaging as complete and total negativity.

In order to have some balance in our lives it is important that we understand negatives and that we can acknowledge them, this is a pattern to look for and try and understand where someone's "positivity" post might be coming from. My take on things is quite clear as I do not wallow or wish to harp on about my son's deaths as this can drum up some real negative concepts indeed. The reason behind it is that in order for any one single thing to be "real" or authentic, to have a very sincere form of being "genuine" then both positive and negative must exist. I have learned this in a very harsh few lessons in my life, there is no reason for you to take my word for it other than I can testify to how a positive feeling feels, I will encourage you to remain as upbeat as possible and to take this viewpoint of life and gain enjoyment in some of the beauty around you. I like to encourage you to work on self and continue to seek out and find the beauty that is around you all of the time. This is something that I encourage as it has been born out of some of the darkest and deepest negatives I have ever experienced. This is a reason that I can attest to the feelings I now have on a daily basis are quite real and genuine. Authenticity is not found on every street corner or every post you see on the Internet. These are the words to the wise, it is good to follow and remain upbeat with some of what is posted online, and it is great that you get a few uplifting moments from time to time. What I hope you do consider or remain understanding about is that there are flaws in us all and without slipping into a delusional state of mind, where everything is all positive all of the time, be careful to check with self from time to time. Find a balance in life and how much of the positivity you take on board as there is always a correction waiting behind closed doors. Nope I am not trying to rain on your parade and introduce negative aspects to any of your positive vibes. The point to consider and to remain aware of is that if you shower yourself with positives to help change around your life then what will happen the next time you have a down day? When your market correction appears, could it be catastrophic? These are things to remain vigilant about when making changes in our lives. When taking steps to pull ourselves out of depression or taking time to mellow ourselves out from overanxious minds. It is important to factor in some balance. The Internet is a great source and so are some books, just like this one (insert smiley face). The power of the positivity is wonderful and far reaching as we all know; I am just mentioning to you to keep a balance between what is going on in front of your eyes on a screen and what is going on in your life. We can become kind of like big fat cookie monsters for positive engagements online and then when we actually do pull ourselves away from the online world we sit alone in the dark and sob to ourselves. Keep a balance where and at all times possible. Look out for the so-called trending themes and those who push them on you as you may find this is only a passing fad. What we are actually looking for is a little pick me up and maybe a touch of support. If you can find some people who generate these kinds of things, then you may be on to more of a safer way to aid yourself in healing or calming or undepressing yourself.

What I found in many places were that there are so many great new sayings that come out, but they carry a lot of like almost the passive / aggressive type tone.

Example,

If you have not done x, y & z then you can only achieve l, m, n, o, p.

Or

It is in times of your most low you will find out your true friends.

So, what is the issue right? Well first off, the idea of having to be experienced and wise to accomplish anything is a bit of no brainer and full of you know what. We humans can accomplish anything once we set our minds to it. An important piece to remember is that if some of the positive sayings bring about the negatives in the first place maybe you have no need to consider such things at all. Remaining upbeat can be all about being upbeat and something negative does not have to be explained just to show you that a positive can occur. Like about finding our true friends when we are low. Well I like to think of all my friends as true friends and introducing the possibility that they might not be as good at keeping me down or stir crazy in the head as I was and I never needed to see a post or the likes of something putting a poor negative spin on things. I always think of my friends as true good friends or they just wouldn't be my friends anymore. I am not in need of a lowly moment to test them, who needs to test their friends? That is why I call them friends in the first place because I find a comfort level with them that suits me in my own selfish taking caring of me way. I do not need a litmus test for my friends.

The point I am kind of saying is that not all help is healthy help and not all that appears positive is sending the right message into your conscious mind. Keep an eye out and remain vigilant and at all times, check in with self. No tangents required just keep an eye out for where you can achieve the most peace and if something is a pressured situation or something is preying upon you for your time and money just because you have appeared a little in need of some positive help in your life, be wary and check with self. Do I need this? Does this fulfill where I am travelling to on my journey of self, right now? Am I benefiting from what I am involved with right how? These are all good check points to take note of and have a little check in with self from time to time to help keep your balance.

This my friends has been a word to the wise from Aidan Mc Nally, brought to you by our sponsor TWO sons TOO many.... lol.

Happier Me

When I say Me, I of course mean we, or at least me for now while I am writing and you for you as you are reading. I am happier though, to be honest. I have had some very angry days in my life and I have come out the other side of them and found a happier me. Do you think perhaps that it is not possible for you? Is becoming a little happier even a possibility like when we are already cruising along at a nice rate of knots, who needs happier anyway, right? I have found that laughter is a great thing to have in our life and sometimes a whole bunch of organized laughter can be a great way to spend a few hours. I was telling you earlier how I had been to a comedy cub not too long ago, well it was a great way to enjoy an evening and just laugh at jokes. There is something in laughter that can keep us going in life. Not only does it warm us up a bit but when we are laughing and sometimes to the point of tears, yup you guessed it we are breathing deeply. But the happy or happier is not something connected to laughter really, I guess it is a little unfair of me to introduce such a topic as being happier with a reference to laughter. The reason that I do was to explain that even through all of my personal gut wrenching and heartache, there was a time I

thought I would never, and I mean never ever laugh again.
The reason I can laugh is because I became happier in life
which then in turn allowed me to laugh. I was once in a place
where if I laughed, I felt guilty, that I had nothing to even
smile about. I was drowning in grief for my sons and how
could I find a time or a place or any scenario to actually laugh?
This would kind of be where and how I learned about our
mind continuing to keep us stuck sometimes, I cannot say it
was easy to shake off, but it definitely had its grip and that
grip has gone away now.

If you are like me and sometimes it is difficult to find the old
you or find the person you thought you were and many of
your days are all seeming to have a little grey in them, then
yes, it is important that we find times to laugh. "laughter is a
great medicine" is a wonderful saying and is one that I cannot
really find any flaw with. Some people will never understand
why some people laugh more than others and others will just
never understand some people. That's not a saying I have ever
heard, that's just all me. When changes have occurred in my
life and some growth type stuff, personal growth has come
about. They always came along with the same fears and
nervousness and they always hurt a little bit. I have found that
isn't it beautiful to be able to hurt? No, I am not sadistic in
any type of way, what I am reaching to is to highlight that in
order to experience happy then I suppose it only makes sense
that we understand sad too. If we do not know a sad place,
then how can we know what a happy place is? Just like the

genuine of negative and positive, in order to be authentic, they must both exist. If you think this is nuts or something, attach only the positive side of your battery to your car, it has all the energy of the power of the battery in the positive post and should quite easily be able to run the stuff you need running in your car. The thing that occurs is that without the negative post also being connected there is no functionality of the vehicle. Both are required to complete a circuit and allow the power to work properly. We are quite like the car, if only an abundance of power supply of positivity can charge us to function, then this would be amazing, however we need em both. We actually need that little bit of negative in our lives to keep us balanced. I will hazard a guess that you may have experienced this once in your life, scenario...

You are all set to watch a movie, you have all your favourite snacks ready and you have the curtains closed. You are making a complete and total cinema experience in your own front room and ready to watch a movie that you have been waiting to see. Have you ever prepared all of this and then ten or fifteen minutes into the movie a tiny peel of light at the top of the blinds grabs your attention? It is just where the curtains meet and they are not quite overlapping properly, this is a tiny bit annoying to you, but you tell yourself it is okay and you do not wish to pause the movie. 35 minutes into the movie and you just cannot stand the gap anymore so you press pause and you go about fixing the fault in the curtains or whatever the distraction is, you then go back to watching the movie. It is now thoroughly enjoyable. We needed the little crack of light to annoy us just enough to take from our movie experience so that when we finally fixed it better that then we were able to enjoy our movie completely.

A happier me does not see the crack of light in the curtains anymore, when I set something up such as, to watch a movie, I now can do it and no matter if there is a bulldozer digging up my front yard or not, it will not deter me or distract me in any way. If I set my mind to watch and enjoy a movie, then that is what I will do.

Once upon a time I used to almost go out of my way to tell the naysayers off, I would make a point to argue with the begrudging people that entered into my life. A simple argument of mine would be to explain to them how if I presented them with a white sheet of paper and told them it is a blank sheet of completely white paper, would they agree? The naysayers among us will look for the smudge of grey or black in the actual manufacturing of the paper, when they see it, they will disagree and claim it is not a complete white sheet of paper. Once they have brought that up it is almost impossible for them to accept that it is in fact a blank sheet of white paper. Some people just like to look for flaws and when they find them, they are like trumpeters to have a parade that they found the flaw. If somebody tells me they have a white sheet of paper and show it to me I will accept their word for it as I am not looking for the flaw. If it is indeed flawed that is for someone else to look for. If I see a sheet of paper that is

99.9% a white sheet of paper, then that is more than satisfactory to me. Some people cannot accept this to be true and so they will spend 99.9% of their focus on that 0.01 percent of black smudge that they have identified. Can this be a happy way to exist? They will argue and rightfully so as they are wishing to have everything 100 percent what it is and 100 percent correct. Is it time that mellows us or just a truck load of self-work that mellows us? I am unsure about this one. Those of us who look for the negatives in any situation will always find them. When we look hard enough, something will appear to us as that is what we are searching for. So, to this point it is a simpler route for me now to see the good, see the beauty and see the white sheet of paper for what it is without any desire for absolute perfection and no desire to find any negative aspect. We can all make great strides in bettering ourselves and it is well worth that we recognize our efforts and not to stay focused on the little bits that we maybe struggle with.

I will and always have looked for the good in people, I usually find it and see the world in a way now that shows me the decency of mankind. I am fully aware of any other aspects that exist and types of people who coexist in this world with me, I do not wish to focus on them or the other side. I will acknowledge all that is negative for what it is however I choose not to focus on it. I have been training myself to look beyond the smudge on the piece of paper and understand that it is a white sheet of paper. The ability to see beyond the smudge comes with a happier me I suppose. How can we gain this ability and what is there for us to use it on in our daily life to help us change for the better?

Having the ability to see beyond any person's flaws can help us to see beyond our own. We know ourselves well and we continue working on ourselves not because it is some 100 % self-perfection that we strive for, no, it is that we can feel very happy in reaching 80 percent or 90 percent of the true person that we are. These are massive steps we have taken in our life to achieve goals that we have set for ourselves and massive steps in the direction that has brought us to a happy place, a place with peace and an eye now for beauty in life around us and in others who we meet.

When we can see that a simple flower is beautiful and was there for us to enjoy at the precise moment, we decided to enjoy it, then this is a happy place. When we can sit in our own company and allow our mind to ease and allow our feelings to surface, then this is a happy place. When we can wake on time and be in to work with some minutes to spare then this is a happy place. When we can rest at night in our bed and feel the cushion of our mattress underneath us and how it almost hugs us and our pillow welcomes our heavy head, then this is a happy place. A happier me or a happier you is a beautiful thing in our world. For every one of you who struggle to find that happy place, I want to let you know it does exist and it is there for you. It will take some practice and some baby steps so to speak to get there perhaps, when you do you will be, a happier me.

I use the word happy not too lightly at all and am aware that many of us never thought we would ever see happy ever again. Content is a word I prefer most of the time and I mention it because I am aware that some of us also may find it quite difficult through different chemical reactions in our body to achieve happy. When we are content at night in our bed, we are in the same state we were in when we were wrapped in a baby blanket as a newborn, this is a beautiful state of mind to achieve and can be just as we were intended to live. We achieve it by being aware of the negatives that exist in our lives, we acknowledge them by understanding they exist, yet we never pay them homage, we do not focus our efforts and our attentions on them as they can only take from us. They can only help to keep us stuck or help to keep us down. For every 1 single negative thing you can think of right now, I ask of you that you begin to think of the positive items too. Begin to focus on the positives in your life, find that appreciation inside of yourself that you are alive and all around you in the world has beauty. It is there if you look.

My friend who works in the field of psychology has explained to me previously that it will take 5 positive comments to counterbalance one negative comment inside of our psyche. For every 1 negative we hear we happen to hold on to them and it takes 5 times as many positives to kind of swoosh them out from our brain.

That would suggest we need to build up around ourselves a ton of more positive affirmations about our life to begin gaining a true happy place. It is important we tell ourselves nice things and if needs be get the sticky post it notes and put them on your refrigerator or around your mirror so that when you see them you are building all the time a strong foundation for yourself to where, when you do find that happier me, you will have no trouble at all in staying there for the long haul.

What can we Do?

Just like our positive and negatives and how we focus on them, we often focus on what we cannot do. This is a normal trait in us humans and we have been hearing for almost all our lives that we have limitations and all of how we cannot do certain things. The main critic for these of course is us and there is not much we can do about any of it, if we should take that attitude.

How can we do some stuff and not do other stuff? What do I mean by stuff? How come we can walk? Because we saw this when we were a baby and we then within a small few months we decided, hey everyone else is doing it so I am going to start. But we were probably not even one year old at the time and why did we want to do it in the first place? Our survival instinct showed us that it is the way to survive in this place, if we wanna get around we better start acting like the rest of them. So, by one year old we have something going on inside of us that is about basic instincts of survival. Yet as adults we have a tough time figuring stuff out in life? Can we revert to being a baby and wipe our memory clean and shut out all that has gone before our very eyes? I do not think so although I have heard of different therapies that can take or remove poorer or "bad" experiences from our conscious and replace them with happier thoughts and feelings. Sounds like a right old brain washing indeed (total recall, eat your heart out).

Without being so drastic as attending therapy to take away some of our less enjoyable times in life, can we find a way to block them out and just forget em? We can of course and many of us do exactly this. We block out the traumas and the hurt as they were not nice and then through time, we have forgotten them like they never existed. We have the ability to lock them deep inside of ourselves and never to be accessed again. Block them out some people will call it. What are we doing by suppressing these such memories? Are we closing off a piece of our life from ourselves? Sometimes some people will act irrationally and not have any proper reasoning for why they act in any certain or particular way. They will say that they have had a history of being troublesome or that they have "always just been that way". Many times, in therapy people uncover some stuff they have locked away inside of themselves and it then unlocks and uncovers to themselves some traumatic times that they experienced. These can be painful for an individual to work through although most people I have ever met have been very grateful that they did unlock the issues and have worked through them as it helped catapult them to a new understanding of themselves and new horizons in their life.

Some will argue that it is best to leave some things untouched and carry on. I am a believer in the purity of life and that its finest form of purity for each of us is inside of ourselves, our own thoughts and feelings are where our complete life occurs for us. It is not outside of ourselves with friends or situations. Yes all of these things do serve as stimulants to our life and how we react but the entirety of what we feel, what we think and how our mind works all happens inside of ourselves, all of our experiences all happen within the same mind that you are now reading these words with.

In order to best serve ourselves or to become the best version of ourselves it would be important that we leave no stone unturned in our self. All answers that we seek from the outside world actually are inside of ourselves. Just like in our dreams when we sleep, how does the dream know where to end up? Do we dream in reverse or something and then run it all backwards like a film reel? As for the dreams, how do they know? Like I have woken up to someone calling me as I have asked to be woken at a particular time in the morning and it has happened that the person calling me tied directly into my dream. I have awoken to a car alarm on the street outside of my apartment before and it was at the precise time that I was in the middle of a dream where a siren was going off in the dream.

How did the dream build me up all along to create something where the sound from the world outside in the awake world coincided exactly and precisely with my dream? If this is the case our mind knows the future. And also when we hear someone say "It will happen for you when the time is right, the time is just not right now" or "everything happens the way it is supposed to happen" is that because our mind knows when the time is right because it has been building us up for stuff all along as it knows the exact time and place for things to happen to us, just like how the outside world ties right into the ending of a dream. How does our mind know this stuff? There is nobody else inside of our heads pressing buttons and making it up as we go along or controlling the shots, so to speak. What can we do about these kinds of things along our journey?

We can continue our path of self-discovery; we can raise all the issues we need to raise and unlock any such traumas inside of ourselves to allow us to grow. If we can get to a state of mind where we are able to turn on and off our thoughts whenever we please then we can take control over them. If we are able to experience all of our feelings from inside of us, then we are able take control over them by how we allow ourselves to act based upon how we feel. We can take control over our own lives and how we will proceed by feeling first and then thinking what we should do about how we feel.

This concept will lead us to a much more pleasant life, and we can accomplish all that ever comes in front of us.

We can put an end to our thinking first and convincing ourselves that we feel any particular way. The path being that when we think first and then tell ourselves how to feel, that this is a possibility of why or how we sometimes have no answer and cannot shake off any negatives and we continue to have a much lowlier feeling all of the time. We are blocking out our feelings by telling ourselves how to feel. Feelings cannot be told how to be or when to arrive, they occur. Thoughts can however be told when to function and when not to function and it is inside of ourselves that we can choose how to think and what to think about. Actors are probably the greatest at this art of being able to think themselves in to mimicking a feeling. They are able to take on a persona and act.

Some of us in the world may have a little, well just a tiny addiction to drama and those of us who do can also act, there are those of us in the world that may not be in any big blockbuster Hollywood movies, even though we sure can act. I learned that by doing the meditation type breathing and that by allowing myself to relax, a whole bunch of feelings can occur, and my thoughts can come to a complete silence. If I was able to achieve this to help me begin to see things clearer, then so could anybody. This is something we can do and then we no longer have to act anymore. This is a complete freedom that I never knew existed. A freedom of expression and an understanding of self that I learned through very deep hurt and sorrow. My pains were killing me inside and I did not have the tools to understand them. I did not know where or how to even begin. To dig through what I was feeling. They were very real feelings and what could be termed extremely raw feelings too. I had to make a very clear decision that I was not going to allow anything inside of my head or coming from my gut emotion, I had to decide that none of this will kill me and I will allow them to flow. Yes, painful however it is something that we can do. No matter how hard you may feel something it will never be more powerful than you in your entirety. There are no thoughts that can shake you down to your knees and make you beg for life. What we can do is take charge over our sorry selves and rebuild. We can take over the process of how we think. Just how when we were babies and we were trained to use the toilet or how we were nurtured along to learning how to chew our food when we eat and not just choke on the first bite, we learn.

What we can do is teach ourselves to be okay with feelings that cause us pain and I am talking about feelings that are so strong that we would just rather not feel them at all. What we can do is begin again in our life, we can put all the horrible behind us and begin slowly peeling away the onion that we have become and just go little layer by layer and allow ourselves the freedom we deserve and quite often freedom that we crave. To be alive in our freedom is such a beautiful thing and there is no place or way I would rather be. My experiences are much tastier now and I love life.

I have used as a promotional tool for a while now in a lot of my own self-promotion or advertising, the word SELF. The letters standing for another meaning too.

Succeed (in all that we attempt in life)

Elevate (lift ourselves up to new heights)

Live (beyond what we have ever even imagined)

Free (from any feelings or thoughts that wish to imprison us)

These are things that we can do for ourselves and by ourselves if we wish to achieve results or have any idea that we wish to make changes in our lives. Nothing is impossible. Anything that we think is holding us back is right inside of ourselves. Unlocking these things can create the wonderful world that we have a hunch exists.

SELF (beyond)

This is wonderful that we can unlock the route to ourselves by dealing with all that goes on inside of self. We can also live free, Succeed, Elevate, Live, Free. This is great to know or to have been introduced to. So how does this benefit our lives? What can we do about learning about ourselves that will all of a sudden make the magic happen? Nothing is the basic answer.

There is no simple key to unlock anything you probably already do not know about yourself. Like I had mentioned before how I found that with all the questions I have had about life, for just as many questions I have had, I have had all the answers also.

When we spend some time in discovery of self we begin to see with a much clearer view of the entire world and everybody in it. There are times we may sound to our friends like a conspiracy theorist as we have taken a whole new view of many things. A light bulb is no longer just a light bulb, we actually begin to understand how it works. Just like everything around us. We begin to see life in technicolor. As another old acquaintance of mine used to say, "life, he can read it like a children's book". These things are quite possible and very beautiful. All stemming from some work on self and learning about ourselves, we unlock so much more to life. Not only because we can begin to truly live in the now of our each and every day, there is so much more to be appreciative of. When we understand ourselves, we realize there is no need for any other to have to understand us. The pressure is off, and we do not have to stay in a rat race where we are always competing. There are no more browsing the Internet to see what is going on everywhere and who is doing what. It all becomes less interesting as we have unlocked a path into ourselves and are allowing self to live free in the world around us. I know it sounds very much the sandals and green tea type stuff of the world and how it is in a sense. It is a great new place where we wish to feel our feet touching the ground. We enjoy feeling the rain on our face and we also love to feel hot sun baking down on us. Nothing can bring us down only ourselves and we have an allegiance to only ourselves, our selfish plan of self-care does work and when we gain this beautiful view of the world and everything in it, it is then that we begin to be able to see others and make attempts to assist them in their own journey of dissecting an issue and helping others realize their own potential. Not only have we unlocked ourselves and began to achieve great new things in our lives, we have left behind us the situations and people that have brought about so much sheltering of us. Some care for us and we have been smothered by them which did not allow us to grow into the person we were born to be.

It is no fault of any persons that they did not see what we see now, it is no fault of any person for trying to love us in the way that they knew how. It takes us on a journey where we now become so free inside of ourselves that everyone that we now meet will not know why they like the shine from us or the glow or the buzz, they will just want some of it too. What is it that can be so powerful that others will want to be like you or have a tiny piece of what you now have? The funny thing of course is you have nothing special or nothing that every person doesn't already have.

How or what is it that they want from you. Having unlocked yourself will be the best thing you have ever done and you will sense with almost a new 6th sense of how some will wish to pull you back to the person you used to be. You will sense those who will wish to knock you down and not try to pull you gently back but who wish to drag you right back to a needy person or a depressed person or someone who just doesn't have it all together. It is not their fault as they are just being the self-invented person, by way of their own years of developing their strategies to hide, that they have become used to being. No person is doing it out of any badness to try and drag you back. There has been a comfort for them in having you the way they needed you to be. To give them their purpose.

Having made strides in personal growth and unlocking some pathways to our feelings and how we now take charge over what we think about how we feel, we have taken a step to a different plateau in life. We begin to see just like I was explaining about the compass before, we can see with 360-

degree vision and there is nothing that can hold us back. No person or situation can bring about any regression to bring us back to being stuck anymore. It is not any person's fault that they behave a certain way around us or towards us. This is all about themselves and not about you. It is the limitations that they are placing upon themselves that are keeping themselves stuck. What you can do with self and by going beyond self is just like a children's book, you can read how things are and you can sense the trapped feelings or the unspoken word among even some of your closest friends. Well even more shocking than that is how you can hear in a stranger's voice or see in a stranger's eyes that they are locked deep inside of themselves. Someone you have never even met before. Imagine that just because of beginning on a road to self-discovery you have now unlocked some almost like mind reader / x-ray specs ability, a vision right into the soul of others too. We do not become clairvoyant or anything special like this, we just simply become aware. Being aware is a natural benefit to have in our lives today. Awareness is something we may have forgotten all about and we were living a little sheltered from many pieces of ourselves.

Probably the finest about ourselves and life is that even though the world is all around us, yet our life is happening right inside of us. When we hear our own thoughts, that is life happening inside of us. When we hear other people's words or we see other situations occur in front of or eyes in the world out there in front of us, it is being processed by our brain right inside of ourselves. We hear and we speak and we think and we feel all from right inside of ourselves. The world beyond self is out there and is only providing to us stimulants that we either react to or do not react to. So really when we can focus on self, then the whole entire world becomes in order and the clarity in which we perceive this world is all clear right here inside of ourselves. Is that just amazing or what? A good time in life can be had all by adjusting ourselves.

The part that makes me want to continue writing and expressing to you forms of things that I have noticed or learned is that I understand that there are many people who suffer from various degrees of pain and hurt along with mental health issues and they may have a feeling of nobody understands them.

I want to reach you and the only format I can do this by is writing it all out for your reading and hope you will get to read with me and take a tiny piece away that gives you hope to succeed in your journey.

It definitely pains me to hear of when someone has taken their own life and it brings no pleasure to my ears nor to my feelings of how if we could reach each other, we could chat or have an exchange to where you can feel for yourself that everything IS possible and life is not a horrible thing or a horrible place. It is only clarity and an awareness of self that has afforded me the ability to see beyond self and realize there are so many of us all the same with only slight differences and when we can find each other out here in the world then we can help each other out. As humans we can afford each other this kind of loyalty to each other and look out for each other in these ways. If you know someone who you think may enjoy reading what I have wrote here then by all means share the hell out of it, tag them in your posts or send them a private message with a link to the book. It is not for me and book sales that I care to reach more and more people. The sole reason is that I wish to reach out beyond self and to reach as many as I can possibly help in any little way to offer them a little guidebook, hand-book to help them gain some little tools to save themselves and their life too.

I fully understand how hard it is and can be and I wish to let all of the world know that there are ways to help us overcome all obstacles that we come across in life.

We ARE the answer to all of our questions.

It is upon self to be ready to commit and to do the work, it is upon self to rise up and learn about your own inner workings. It is self who will fully reap all the benefits and it is self who can then help do more for others too. This is what I like to call self and going beyond self. When we discover how we can be okay and we can have a life without misery then it is only right that I share with as many as I can that it is possible, I am living proof of why and how. Share with your friends, help them to become aware of self too. These kinds of things are going beyond self, not just for me but for a friend out there who may need it too. We are all humans, all of us. We all deserve every chance we can get at becoming a tiny little piece more content in the world we live in.

We all were born to deserve everything, yes some of us are more fortunate than others and some of us have nothing by way of material things. What we can do and we are most deserving of is a peace in our minds and a heart that can love, both giving and receiving.

You, me and everybody deserves to have a shot at bringing to their life some breathing to help ease their minds and their emotions. Once we have gained an awareness of Self, then there will be times we may benefit greatly by going beyond self.

Challenges & Changes for the good

There is so much in our lives that sometimes it can be hard to take it all in or take stock of what exactly is going on with us inside of ourselves. People around us have needs too and we cannot just shut ourselves off because we are deciding to do a little inner work on ourselves. We are faced with challenges everyday by the world around us because there are our other commitments like family and neighbours and close friends who all want to have a little slice of the pie from time to time. Where can we find any time to begin to focus on ourselves? Some of the challenges and perhaps a very large one is finding the time to just head off and do some meditation. We may find it hard to steal 4 minutes out of our day to practice our deep breathing, how can we find the time?

Finding time is not an easy one to figure out at all and now that our lives are so busy and everyone is in close contact with everyone all of the time, should we try and take a little time out, it is possible every what's app group in the world will have an APB out on you in no time at all. So how do we juggle our life now that we have entered into some self-discovery? I guess we can begin by minimizing how much time we spend on our phone. We could try and discipline ourselves into a new habit of 30 minutes every evening will be ours. Thirty minutes is not a lot of time to set aside for ourselves. As a matter of fact, it is a tiny little amount of time and a lot less than we actually deserve. We deserve easily two or three hours of me time in each day and this could be a way to really slow things down. Let's just say, providing we can find the time to do the time we need to breathe and slow everything down to a snail's pace for a half an hour each evening. Do you think you are worth thirty minutes? I firmly believe that you are worth much more but it is very understandable that life is still happening around us so a thirty-minute time slot may be all that we can manage. If we want results then it is important that we manage to find the time, substitute something of lesser importance, this should be easy because nothing is really more important than you and so find a way to face the challenge of time, first off.

While thinking of challenges and now that we have agreed that you are so important to your life that you have thirty minutes to spare, what other challenges could we face? Ahh yes, the changes that come over you within your first week even. How can we deal with everyone around us when a change is coming over us in our life? Will the children know who this new person is that is showing up every day now and being more involved? Will our partners recognize that something different is going on with us and will they begin to mention it? People at work and in all areas of our life will notice that change is coming over us and it may upset their apple tart a little. Not everyone is for a new you, remember that.

Some will want the old you just the way you are as they have become very used to you and do not know how their own world is going to be if you go and just start making changes to yourself. The challenges are so far, about how other people may react or find it weird or different that you take time for yourself, what do we say about other people? (fuck em) nah just kidding. We must remember that this is a selfish way to improve self. The selfish portion of it means that there is no other person more important than self so to try and accommodate others is something that we cannot bother to entertain.

If we wanted to really see a movie in the cinema then we somehow find the time to do that. It will be a little easier than you first think to actually find the time to slow your day down and take time for yourself.

What if I become emotional as I do my relaxation and I am all teary eyed when I return to my family life? What will the children think if they see me crying a little bit? My children are not used to seeing me cry and so I am not sure it is a good idea to practice these exercises of relaxation around them. That is fine, just wait until they have gone to bed. Other than that, it is just part of working on our ourselves and the changes which will become are changes for the good so we can do it as we know that our goal is totally worth the journey of allowing our children see us emotional.

These changes are for the good of our own life and then in turn can enrich the lives of people around us, it is by simple steps daily that we are bringing about small change to our lives. Speaking to ourselves in front of the mirror in the mornings. Post it notes all around our kitchen, these are things we do not have to hide. When our partner hears us giving ourselves positive reinforcements as they drive along in the car, at first, they will think something weird is going on and then they will begin to see that the changes are working and slowly but surely, they will want to become involved too. Changes for the good of ourselves are easily sniffed out by others and though they will not be able to place their finger on what it is you have started doing in your life, they will want to know something. The real challenges will more than likely be about what is going on, on the inside of ourselves. How we begin to deal with feeling nicer ourselves on the inside. This can be something so new and rare that we find it hard to accept ourselves.

What exactly can change about ourselves that might become so scary and all wonderful just by being a little gentler on myself and taking on some practices of how I speak or what I say to myself. How would anybody ever see the difference? Oh, believe me you will now stick out like a sore thumb and when you do, it can be fine to share a little of how you have been reading this book and this and that and this and that.

When they ask for a loan of the book you will be saying, nah not going to happen as this is like my hand book and when I want to go back to a piece and read it again, I will have to keep my copy handy. Tell em get their own copy cause no loaning out of this one.

All change is scary and for some strange reason we try to avoid changes as much as possible. Like in physical change as we grow, there are the things known as growing pains. You have heard of these, they are muscular pains a young teenager may experience when their muscles are stretching and they are growing, quite often in the large muscle of the thighs. So growing pains are something that actually exist in the physical, we fear growing pains of the emotional as we do not want to hurt or feel any pain. The scary part of change is a fear of the unknown or a fear of feeling different. Change in one's self cannot occur without growth, by growing we naturally change. This is an awesome way in which to discover new stuff about ourselves and can be an adventure of discovery. As with any adventure / journey it can be exciting and on the edge of your seat type stuff, this is not anything to be scared of, excited yes, nervous maybe, scared nah. A feeling of something scary in our life is all natural and is important to allow the feeling through, we will often find that underneath the scary pieces are other emotions that are simmering away and at the surface of it all is a little fear and nerves, down a layer or two more inside of our emotions factory and we can discover new feelings that are coming through too. Letting go of anxiety and nerves can allow some of the real you come to the fore. Sometimes when we are feeling raw emotion and something new has come up for us, we feel like others can see right through us like we are see through and our vulnerability feels like we are totally naked, we have a big wide window into our inner sanctum and we cannot shut it or there are no blinds to draw over so that we can keep people out, even a little. These feelings of exposure to the world can be part of why we avoid changing too much and sometimes are the reasons for us to stall our own growing until we find a time to become more comfortable. This is all normal and are all part of changing for the good of ourselves.

You probably have heard friends say before that they "feel bored and a change would do them good" so they up and move to a new apartment. People will say things like "oh I need a change of scenery" and even in the 12-step program of AA the big book as they call it mentions clearly how "geographical changes mean nothing". We can change our clothes, our car, our apartment, our hair, our jobs, the country we live in, our name (if we like) all of these bring about some temporary relief to how we feel. The change that is everlasting is change on the inside in our emotional well-being. This is the stuff that can last a lifetime and you will enjoy it so much that the little fears that have prevented you so many times will now become laughable. I say "little fears" not to minimize how you may feel. It is only to help you practice seeing them as little. I totally understand that fear can feel so huge that it is the monster that sleeps under you bed and all day every day it feels like it is coming for you and you cannot stop it. So, we run and hide as often as we can. These are ways to block out our fear and to continue on a survival path of plodding along. Emotional challenges and changes for the good of yourself are probably the best gift you will ever give yourself and for this reason I encourage you to begin to see the fear as little.

The changing of all things on the outside does not last for long and when we begin working on our self on the inside and begin to feel the lasting change, we may become a little addicted even and want to change everything more rapidly. Remember how our dreams know how to tie everything together in the right way so the middle is the middle and the end is the end, this is also the case of our emotional health and well-being, slowly and steadily is how, somehow our mind already knows. We will question things and have no answer, rest assured that the answers are inside of ourselves and as we continue peeling back the layers just like the onion, we will reveal to ourselves at the right times the answers we have sought at previous times in our lives.

The ever so popular saying of "there is nothing to fear but fear itself" it makes a lot of sense and along with all the sayings and clichés, they all make sense if and when we slow our life down to read em and begin to see em clearly. Any fears of change are a hindrance, though they are very real, they prove to be the spanner in the works from the beginning and once we minimize them and take away any power, they have over us, then the real party starts. When we see fear as just something that is getting in the way and is holding us back, we can slowly begin to minimize it and then we start to realize how that saying is so perfectly right and correct, the only fear of what? Was the actual fear itself.

If the seasons never changed in mother nature around us, we possibly would never know what it is like to experience the depths of winter into the blossoms of summer. The plants and animals do not fear these changes. They all have techniques and have adapted to how the cycle of life keeps on going. We humans on the other hand have created things like escaping to avoid change or blocking out feelings to continue without any fear or worries. If these methods work for you, I do applaud you and at the same time I plead with you to allow a few attempts to bring forward your feelings and begin to live somewhat a simpler life. Simple in the terms of less complicated and without the head hurting of always being in your thoughts.

Change can hurt

Change is inevitable

Change is growing

Change is good.

Please repeat these every so often, you will know when. Changes are a wonderful piece of us growing. We grow anyway as we continue on a journey since day 1. Why not help ourselves and embrace, CHANGE.

THE WORDS WE USE DAILY

Life just keeps happening all around us and we have no magic wand to ever stop it for a minute and take a break. People continue to move forward all around us and sometimes it can feel like everything everyone says is hurtful to us in one way or another. There are times when we are a little more vulnerable and sensitive to every little thing around us and we try to even avoid some people because of how they use their words. Again, it is a good time to point out that nobody is trying to be hurtful towards you and it may just be that your sensitivity has been heightened a little and so it feels like things people say are just so totally insensitive. They do not mean it usually.

What is most important are the words we use when we are speaking, both to ourselves and to others. We have heard people comment about others of how "oh they just love the sound of their own voice" this is something we understand and if we think about it for a moment and what it could mean. The person loves to be heard and is always taking the opportunities to speak out loudly among a crowd or in a group, they want to hear themselves talk. Well guess what? We all hear ourselves speaking and the words we use every day when talking are not only being delivered to whomever we may be speaking with, they are also being heard by ourselves. As we speak there is a slight mumble or murmur that runs up our neck somewhere on the inside just below our ears. Not only are we hearing the words that we are speaking we are physically feeling them occur right at the time that we are speaking. We hear every word that we say. The words that we use can be a huge difference in our own journey. Not the words we intentionally whisper to ourselves in times of relaxation or the words we speak to ourselves in front of the mirror when speaking to ourselves. The words we use on a daily basis are constantly being heard by ourselves. A funny piece may be when we are talking at somebody else and we might say "they aren't even listening" and we are not being heard. Who is the most important person on your journey? You, yes. That is correct, you are the most important person and so when speaking with others or at others, we are hearing every single word we say also. Such use of words and choosing how we speak can make the amount of difference that it is unbelievable that we may have been our own worst enemy for many years of our life.

It is possible to be feeling down and disrespected by another and we tell ourselves how the other person treats us with no respect at all. How they speak to us is disrespectful and we deserve more than this. We deserve respect and we are going to demand it of them. This is fine as it is from another person, we are seeking the respect and we have justified to ourselves in our mind that they should speak to us better and show us some respect. Now what if I suggest to you that you take the same approach to how you choose your own words on a daily basis? Can you take the same approach as to demand a little respect from yourself? Is it possible for you to choose words every day that help reinforce the positivity in your own life? Remember every single word we speak is heard by our "SELF". I will give you an example,

I have avoided as many times as I could possibly the use of the word "but" in the last 300 or so pages. I know I used it a few times here and there and it was totally on purpose that I tried to avoid its usage, "but" is a handy word to use in places and can tie a sentence together real easy, it is the beginning of an excuse and if we are to find and use excuses all of the time we will never get anything done. This was a choice I made some time ago not to allow for the use of the word "but" in my vocabulary. It creates a kind of avenue to an excuse that people will use to get out of something or to sidestep an issue. I do not use it; well I try not to use it as often as possible as I do not wish to sidestep or make excuses for one thing or another. Another is when we use the word "hate", how can we use this word so freely? Someone might say "oh I hate when there is a load of traffic" seems innocent enough and cannot be so strong or hurtful as to tell another person "I hate you right now". It is of course the same word though and I have tried for a long time to not use the word "hate", I find such a strong little word has a lot of power to it. If we hear ourselves saying the word hate it can have a damming effect inside of our mind, we do not need to have such a word in our mind and yes you are correct in the fact that it is I who have introduced the word here in our chat. Hearing ourselves say this kind of word only builds on some negative reinforcement inside of our mind. What could we choose to use instead? I dislike when there is traffic or when speaking to another person, I am not very fond of you right now, these are choices we can make. Even though we are saying a similar thing, we are making a nice word negative by using dis-like, like is still in there and this is a better practice to help how we are hearing ourselves. Saying I am not very fond of you is a way again to use the nicer word fond and turn it negative with the word not. These words and using them these ways still express the same sentiment only when our ears and our mind are listening, we will more than likely hear the nice words too. So, isn't it a lot nicer to hear like and fond when expressing such sentiments of not being too satisfied?

Our mind is listening all of the time, how we use our words is so important to how our overall health and wellbeing can be. There are tons of examples, perhaps too many to cover here at the end of a book, I would need to bring about a whole new book.

There are posts that go around social media these days that explain in a very simple way this exact point, "the person we speak to most in our life is? Yup it is ourselves. So, say nice things".

Did you know that many people have extremely bad habits when speaking? Oh god what a shocker lol. Seriously though, they do. I could have said just there, "No, but seriously they do". This is the point about if you listen, so many people begin a sentence with "No" it is amazing to hear and now that I have introduced it, you will begin to notice it more.

Example of a conversation.

John. I was going to peel the potatoes for dinner later, do you have any preference for what you would like for dinner?

Anne. Ahh it's fine whatever you wanna do will be okay.

John. No, I mean I am asking you what would you like to have?

Anne. No, it's fine whatever you choose.

John. Okay I will make some chops and spuds so if that is okay with you?

Anne. Like I said I do not care one way or the other. If you want, I can make my own if you are busy.

John No, I am asking cause I wanted to know, I have loads of time.

What do our ears hear when we are speaking like this? We hear the word "NO" a lot and we also hear pieces that are negative "I do not care" we are also hearing "whatever" these words and phrases all would need to have some counteracting words somewhere throughout the day to remove them from our mind. The conversation could go

John. I am making some dinner; do you have any preference?

Anne. That is great, I will like anything that you decide to make.

John. Okay, I am open to your suggestions of what you like?

Anne. I am totally fine with making my own if you are caught for time.

John. I am fine for time and I am looking forward to some chops and spuds.

Anne. Great, I will look forward to them too. Yum, delicious.

John. Sorted so, see you later.

A similar exchange of words relaying the same message just not using the words that might fester inside of our minds. It is a simple example to show how making small choices in the words we use can still deliver the same conversation and leave out the pieces that are automatically negatives. Our brain is listening all of the time and when we are being mean or cruel to someone with our words, it is not only the intended person who we are targeting that is receiving the tongue lashing, we are hearing them as well. How do we bring about changes in this area of our life? We begin to replace words in our vocabulary, we use different words to say the same things. Instead of using the word "but" we can find alternatives, however or also or it would be possible for me to do this however I may be a little late and not get around to it. This sounds like a long version of speaking "BUT" it works. Hahahaha.

When I speak out loud or to myself, I try to remain conscious of what words I am using and when at all possible I will catch myself and use alternate words to maintain a nice flow of nice words in what my ears and mind are listening to. It is from choosing my words that I can maintain a nice positive vibe inside of my mind. When we become aware of the words that we are using and being kind to ourselves by better word choices in how we speak, we become aware of how others are speaking too. It is like an epidemic and so much negativity spewing everywhere. Our own awareness is all we can be responsible for, well maybe our children too, we do have a large hand in how they will speak so it is good to teach them early.

The effects of speaking clearly and using words by choice is a great way to maintain a positive upbeat motion to our journey in life, we recognize how others are speaking too and we now have so much stored up in our own positive storage that others words become less powerful and have less effect upon us. We can become immune to negativity altogether. All of this by just altering some of our own words. Is it really possible? I am merely putting it out there for you to try and see how it works for you. Imagine actually becoming immune to the effects of negative people and negative words? That would be amazing wouldn't it?

Another simple technique to assist in creating a fuller and nicer life for ourselves. All we have to do is swap a few words around when we are speaking because when we speak, we are actually hearing everything we say. The other people we are speaking to are so caught up in their own world that they are only catching about half of what we are saying. When we begin choosing our words when we speak you will notice that others are now paying full attention. Their own mind also likes to hear nice kind words and yes this all becomes a little contagious too. Our minds like nice soft words, we like positives and we like to hear nice things. This stands then to reason that if we choose to use words that are nicer, our day becomes nicer, people around us deal with us and treat us nicer and in one simple day our life can become less tiring, less filled with negative and an all-around nicer day. Leaving us feeling fresh and able to take our evening time out and relax in a much more pleasant way. Fascinating isn't it?

The use of our words is a tiny change to make, probably a very valuable technique. Should you be someone who has to make presentations at work and must deliver sales pitches or anything of the sort, you will know full well that there are certain keywords that you will use in your delivery. The word you will use to "hook" a client and other words to not lose a sale. These are techniques used in business and used by professionals who even write presidential speeches for example. Their words are chosen oh so carefully so as to deliver and have the highest impact. Just like those who choose and use words for a living, we are allowed to reap the benefit of choosing our words too. Our benefit is not for financial gain in a job or to win over the hearts of voters on a political campaign. Ours is to sooth our own heart and mind. To continue to be nice to ourselves and allow our emotions to flow freely, our goal and our aim is to win over ourselves. When we have discovered more about self, we can begin to introduce self to the world and let me tell you the world is waiting and ready to receive you with open arms.

Never underestimate the power of your words, the power of how we use them and when we use them. Because we are focused on self and the discovery of self, our words mean everything to us. It is important to remember that how we speak at all times is what we hear, we can choose our words so carefully that we will be wound up tight like an elastic band on one of those foam airplanes. Probably better we make subtle changes and do it gradually to allow ourselves a little time to get used to the new ideas and new version of ourselves. We are not in any rush to achieve and a slow building foundation for ourselves can be an everlasting one.

Once we begin changing our words and we feel the effects of how powerful they really are, it will be like this massive eye opener and something we will find hard to understand how we have not done this sooner. Sometimes we will be in a situation where our words will not be appreciated and there is no need for us to lower our tone to suit those around us. And then other times there will be times where best to just say nothing. Another saying for ya "if you have nothing good to say, then say nothing". Should you ever feel the need for a balance and the ying and yang & day and night & the tide coming in and going out all feel out of whack, go have a screaming session and let out as much of it as you can to balance. There will be times that we will hold our tongue because we have become conscious of how we choose our words and we rather to say nothing than to be hurtful to another, remembering that it is more than likely we will be hurtful to ourselves because we are listening too. It is okay to have a session of letting out all that we have held in, it is actually a little healthy to have a complete blow off of steam sometimes. It is suggested that we do it in a controlled and safe environment like therapy as the therapist can provide us with a safe control to return us back to ourselves and not leave us all depleted and sore.

Amazing that words can do so much for us and can remove so much too. I like to think in a positive tone in my mind and I like to speak as often as I can with nice words. You should try this as often as possible and by being aware that it is you who is listening the most, then it makes most sense to be even sometimes a little over the top and super nice as we all deserve this too.

I am glad you have read this far and that you are seriously considering some changes in your life. I can only assure you that you will have the best of time by adapting some little techniques into your daily living and keeping in mind that it is a coming together of all aspects of these exercises that can complete you to be a very healthy and happy person. Happy and healthy is a beautiful way to feel and when feeling these others begin to feel it too.

There is so much to look forward to on our journey that it is really super to actually feel alive and well. Our words and how we use them in our everyday life have a massive impact and you too will find how beautiful this is. It all only takes a few minor changes along our day to day routine and the benefits are beyond our dreams and beyond how we could ever have envisioned our life to be.

Feeling good

Isn't it oh so nice to be feeling good in life, I mean all the times there are to be upset and feeling down about one thing or another? Some of us strive very hard to feel good and it takes a lot of work. When it doesn't just come naturally easy to a person to feel good, we often say there is something wrong. Saying something wrong, cannot be right, right? Like in how we use our words and all, to say there is something wrong with a person is an awful way to consider another human being. There may not be everything right with you or you may have some conditions or issues that prevent you from feeling good, it definitely does not make you wrong. There is nothing wrong with you. Perhaps we should repeat this,

There is nothing wrong with me.

When we go around saying things like "I don't know what is wrong with me, I just feel exhausted & tired all the time" our listening device is picking up on the word "wrong" and it is applying it to ourselves because we are saying it with "me".

There are situations where some people actually do have particular conditions where they are unable to feel good much of the time. Something like depression can be combated and turned around, when there is a condition or lack of hormone production or thyroid imbalance, it is possible that a person does not possess the ability to stay happy for long or finds it hard to feel good on a daily basis. Should you find yourself in this kind of position it would make sense to discuss with your doctor and seek out some medical advice as there are possibilities that with some hormone replacements or other medical treatments that you can feel happy and may not have to depend on more serious pharmaceuticals. We cannot just make ourselves feel happy just for the sake of it either. Although a natural assumption can be that feeling happy is feeling good. These are two different things in my book (insert smiley face).

Feeling good can come from a number of different situations around us in our lives. We can share in another person's joy and feel good for them and feel good inside of ourselves for being involved. We can feel good for someone and their achievement or they just had a new baby and we feel good for them and with the situation as well. We may ourselves have been having a bad day and have been feeling a little crap and yet it is possible to feel good for someone else's news or joyous occasions. I found it hard for a long time to feel good about anything after my children had died, yet I got moments where I felt good about situations or things that were occurring in my friend's lives. I found that I was unhappy as a general undertone of a feeling, yet I found happiness in other people's joy. The moments were short lived and I returned to my own misery promptly is what I found. I gave it a lot of thought as to what it was that I was missing. Of course, I was missing my children and I was missing them in a sense that is not even possible to put into words, though I was thinking of what is there in my system of feelings that is missing. What piece of my internal workings had gone off the boil? Maybe you ask yourself some similar questions from time to time too. What I found was that it was my own heart ache that was shrouding everything. I was unable to feel much by way or fully feel because my own feelings were covered in an ongoing misery saga. Sounds like it could be called depressed, I wasn't depressed. I was sad. There were fun occasions and birthday parties to attend and even my own birthday party. I didn't want it to happen because I was not feeling like I could fake a smile for too long. I had learned how to fake a smile for short term things like someone else's birthday party and maybe even a friend's child's birthday or something, not my own though. I struggled with understanding what exactly was going on inside of myself. I knew the undertone was a sadness inside of myself and I knew that happiness was a possibility in my life again though I could not join the dots. How can we make ourselves happy if we are suffering? This was basically the question that landed me at a break-through.

I began to write things down. As I sat writing my story out, I went through some of the emotions as well as the memories. It was all, not so easy, for sure and some of what I found was that by crying my eyes out as I wrote allowed me to step away from my desk and feel like I had accomplished something. I had no idea of what as I was not writing a book or anything. I was just writing it all out to help me to understand what it was that had occurred in my life. I have always believed in writing stuff down as a way to remember it, even times when I would write stuff and repeat it to myself as I am writing, this allows me to engage more senses in the process. I am writing, which is using my hands, I am speaking it out, so I am talking and listening to it all at the same time along with thinking about the words also. This engaging the senses has proven to me to work some magic on helping me study for exams or just all round remember stuff. When I began writing as a way to dig through some of my own story and the feelings that came up from time to time about one experience or another, I went from laughing to crying and everything in between.

What I did find was that I walked away from my desk feeling good about the thirty or forty pages I had written and even though I was still a sad person I managed to find a way in which I actually felt good again. Of course I am not saying that writing is for everyone and I am not suggesting that I have a magic formula for feeling good, I am however suggesting that in taking on a little project in our lives we can perhaps see immediate results and these little things can help bring us to a place in our day where we feel good about our own efforts. All doom and gloom can definitely prevent us from feeling good about stuff and little achievements can be a great way to aid us in finding a level to where we can begin to feel good.

Sadness in me stems directly from losing my children and I understand also that perhaps you have not had this experience in your life. There are however similarities between us that have brought us together. We have found ourselves tired of feeling like crap and we want to take some steps on improving this. Achieving goals can be a simple and easy task for you and so if this does not provide stimulation for you to begin to scratch the surface of feeling good. It does not have to be writing that you can turn to, to bring about a little introduction to feeling good in your world.

Plant a rose bush, care for it each day. Allow a tiny piece of your time every day to water it and keep the weeds away from it. Take some time each day to care for it and as the bush grows and you then are the recipient of a beautiful flowering rose you can begin to feel good about why you did it and how it has worked for you.

Perhaps you live in an apartment and do not have a garden. Plant a little window box planter and put some herbs in it. Again, take a little time each day and care for it. When you finally are plucking some herbs and cooking with them you will feel a great sense of achievement and a feel-good feeling can come over you that you once thought was not possible.

The little things in our lives like a flowering plant and a little herb garden/planter box can be enough to show us how our journey is going. Like me with writing, when I started, I did a little piece every day, I saw the results stacking up in page counts and word counts and then eventually I had this massive manuscript to do what with? I had no idea to be honest. It turned out to be my first book and a special monument to my children. Just like you will find that when you eat from your own herb garden, a satisfaction or when you are able to sit and enjoy your rose bush at the time when it is in bloom. I enjoy when someone writes a review of my book or another great one is when I receive a message where someone says "I am reading your book & OMG, I love it" these are great accomplishment feelings and even through my own dark sadness I have experienced this great feeling of feeling good.

Other ways of feeling good are to treat ourselves to some simple things. Leaving aside the projects and aiming for some achievement type satisfactions. Eating a nice meal can be a great way to sit back and feel good. These are all parts of helping ourselves and taking upon ourselves some self-care and helping us to feel good. There is no written right or wrong way to help you begin to feel good and it does not have to be exclusively about yourself. You can feel good about a friend's news or a friend's new baby or whatever the piece is that helps you get a tiny feeling of feeling good then it is worth it. You do not have to be happy and there are no reasons to place harsh rules upon yourself that you must feel this way or that way and if you do not then something isn't working properly and on and on can go the mind. Relax and take the little pieces when you can. The more of them you can manage from time to time are great ways to begin letting feeling good become a habit, once you have developed a habit of feeling nice things and feeling good about them then the habit is something that will stay and run on a kind of auto pilot. There is no correct way and someone like me even found that while feeling shit and living a very miserable and tough mental battle with what was going on. I found ways in which to begin to feel good about myself again. The happiness had nothing to do with it.

Through time though I began to feel good more often and even dipped my toe into the pool of feeling happy. Slowly but surely things began to turn and I was able to feel good and feel happy all at the same time. It didn't mean that I missed my children any less or anything, I had just become okay with missing them and allowed myself to smile again. I began to be okay with feeling good and not trying to convince myself to be guilty for having a smile on my face.

When we develop a habit of feeling good, we can continue along and work on other stuff while we are okay with our feelings and we understand that feeling good comes and goes and is not the B all end all of life, we do gain an appreciation for both our sadness and our happiness.

Feeling proud of somebody close to us, maybe a child or your own child even, feeling proud of them or a friend perhaps or a brother or sister, niece or nephew is a great way to feel a nice feeling and something good. To share in another's moments can be a great way to ease ourselves into the new way of feeling.

There is always the possibility that you have been feeling down and miserable for way too long and keep in mind that the new ways of feeling good and happy and nice things can be so foreign to us that this can be where the scary comes from. It is not like a horror movie or anything that we are scared for short term, we can be scared about how we feel. After all we have been developing these feelings for a long time, how can we just all of a sudden begin to "change" them? I again suggest that the concept of knowing that no new feeling is going to gobble you up and consume you completely. This is something to know and be sure of, this can help allow us to permit the new feelings to occur and we can go with them. Although new feelings can feel strange to us, it is definitely okay to give feeling good a fair shot. There is enough pain, hurt and sorrow out in the world to help you feel miserable for fifty lifetimes, these are easy to slip in to. Funny how feeling good and having a new lease of life for ourselves can be so hard to come to terms with yet we can turn on any news broadcast any day and get enough misery to bog us down for months.

So, what can we do about feeling good? Or how do we accept it? When others around us are still stuck in their misery or their hurt. An important part to also remember is that feeling good is about ourselves. We cannot take away another person's pain and all we can offer is that we become the person who is the bright spark of nice things in their ears. We must continue on our selfish quest to heal self and enjoy our own life before we can even begin to make an attempt to help another. We in our minds may seek out others to comfort them because we crave the miserable feeling ourselves. Of course, it is normal. It is normal because we have spent so much time feeling miserable ourselves that it only stands to reason that we might miss it a little bit. We are totally fine with feeling good and it is an awesome place to have come to in our journey. We do not have to remain up tight and nervous that we might lose our newfound feelings. We also can remember how what feeling down was like, now you compare the two. Which is nicer and which helps you feel alive?

For so long we have felt bad or down and miserable and everything in life seemed like a struggle. This can be what our memory has formed as like a "norm" like memory foam. Our mind has factored in that in order for us to feel normal we must feel a little down. We have become so used to it that we have a harder time feeling good than we do feeling bad. How do we combat this? We flip it and train ourselves to have a new "norm" this new norm now has a standard a little higher that helps us to understand that feeling good is our base that we work from and all above that is absolutely wonderful, all that is below that is below our new norm and we will do our best to make sure that we bounce back to our standard new norm of feeling good more often than not. If you do indeed cherish miserable and have no desire to bring about great new changes, I do wish you all the best and I hope that you will change your mind once you have given feeling good a go. I do believe that once we have conditioned our mind to accept a new level of "normal" that we then slowly but surely begin to see more beauty. We begin to see the nice in people and we begin to live and breathe with just a tiny little bit more ease. This new ease is like taking a long bath and starting over. We can feel weight lift from off of our shoulders. A new normal for us was something we perhaps never even factored a possibility in our lives.

Although when we give it a go, we can find so many things have just automatically changed for us. How we speak with others, how we see our day and the one real fascinating and wonderful piece is of how we feel more often. We begin to feel better.

Feeling better is something at one time in my life I never considered even possible. I am now writing this to you to encourage you to try it as not only did I find a way of feeling better, because it is so awesome I wish for all of the people who suffer in silence to have a slice of it and see that it can be enjoyed.

Other People

Feeling good about ourselves is a wonderful place to be. Yes, we will find it all a little too abnormal for the first while, it will grow on you though and you will wear it with great pride as it is you who knows where you have come out from. It is you who knows what torment and torture you have put yourself through over the years. No other people may understand why you are so happy or upbeat and no other person will ever know what torturous place you have spent your time in. What can other people do for us though in our journey of self? How can we use people in a way that is not damaging to them or to ourselves? We can use others to help us and without them even knowing it. We can use people and their joyous occasions as a way in which to start trying out how we can feel good again, we get happy or joyous about their accomplishments and we can feel proud of them. This is a great technique to try out how we feel. Others will not understand how you have spent nights crying to yourself or how you stayed up all night watching nothing on TV and just kept changing channels. Others will not understand what it has been like to feel so miserable that you ever considered to end the whole entire thing. No others will know these pieces of you and there is no stamp across your forehead to let them know of these things either. You do not have to tell them if you do not wish to as discussing inner secrets are best kept for a select few. Your therapist is a good place to confide in. That is another arena that other people around you will not understand, "why do you go to therapy?"

Your journey is not for other people and it is something to be clear about in your mind, yes, your entire mind. Your spirit and your feeling self along with your brain and all of your senses. It is important to know that there are times where other people serve as a purpose to your healing and becoming the mighty you that you were born to be. The yardstick upon which you measure your success is based upon yourself and not by other people and most definitely not other people's yardsticks of how they measure things in life. Take a look at the roses that you planted and see are they being cared for the way in which you intended or your herb garden, have a quick glance at it from time to time and see if it is being cared for. These are items that will let you know if you have been staying on track or not. It is not other people who will be a benchmark for you because as you change in your life so will your friends. Not that they will change with you, there is a chance you will develop new friendships with like-minded people. New friendships, when you meet new friends who are on a level of understanding with you, it is not that old friends are any less or worse at all. Some other people cannot understand. Having expectations of others will bring about situations where you will be hurt and let down by other people. You do not use them in any kind of sly way or with any kind of malice towards them. You are surviving and looking out for your own well-being. This is the beauty that you will find that other people will now either accept the new you or they will not.

Other people can have very cruel ways which will not tie into your own self-improvement. They may wish to jump on your coat tails so to speak and become like a boat anchor. They will not want to see you fly high and may wish to sit on your back as you begin to journey on, on your pursuit of happiness. These types of other people you may have to let go of and you may have to let go of them in such a way that it is with much of your love for them. Building a better life for yourself is not about bringing along passengers and until you can fly high and be content then you most definitely have no room for passengers.

Other people may not know what they do and how they continuously make attempts to ridicule you or have some sly digs at you about your newfound self and these things can be hurtful. It is not their fault that this is their way. They wish for the old you back because when you were down and stuck and you were always needy you may have given them purpose to look out for you. You may have been their pity pot and as long as you were the one who was needing caring for and looking after, you were serving a purpose to fulfill their needs. The time has come to spread your wings and begin to fly, and you cannot be the pity pot of anybody's anymore.

Other people can be masters at doing the weirdest things to try and help keep you stuck. It is with a deeper understanding of self that you can determine and see clearly how things manifest themselves by the work of others. It is amazing the extent some will go to just to keep you in the dynamic that they believe you belong in. Do not fear setting yourself free as you will find new friends and there are people out there who not only wish to see you fly high, they will also be ready to give you a leg up even higher when they can. There are other people in this life that can recognize your struggles and they will not wish to be passengers; they will encourage you and some are so supportive of you even knowing the journey you are on is one that they cannot come along with you on. Good people exist in the world and bad people exist in the world. There are those who will step on your back to get to the next rung on the ladder of rescue ahead of you and balancing that out are the people who will extend a hand of friendship, they will reach down on that ladder and assist you to climb higher and even put you across their back if they can to help you get to another rung higher.

Some present themselves as the helping hand and turn out to be the opposite. Some represent the boat anchor who wish to keep you stuck and they may turn out to be the most helpful. It is hard to know which is which. When you align your thoughts and your feelings, and your mind becomes clear you will begin to recognize which is which sooner and not have to waste as much time learning as you grow.

You do not judge other people is probably the safest way to proceed as you will find that many times someone is only acting in the way they know how. Most of the time when someone is doing something that is upsetting to you, there is a very good chance they didn't even know they were doing it.

We are tasked with figuring out which is which and who is who all along our journey of self. Do no fret it or give it too much time, things like these become obvious fairly soon. When you see a situation for what it is, it is then your time to make a decision. Base your decisions on your own health and well-being first. If there is something you can benefit, then by all means stick with them. If it is the case that you see there is no benefit and only a continual situation of hurt and ill health, then you know what to do. Turn on your heels and let the door hit you on the way out. You are not being bad in anyway by putting self-first and you need not try to use it as an excuse to bring yourself back down. Your journey is a selfish one and your own emotional, mental and physical health and well-being come first and foremost in this journey of self in our lives.

When you have found your own strengths, you can then begin to extend that hand of friendship to others only learning to fly, just as you gained an appreciation for those who helped you along your journey, when your wings were not so great. There will be a few crash landings perhaps and all the good new friends you make along the way will be there to cushion those landings for you. Do not, out of only fear hold yourself back anymore. Fly high and soar to great new levels in your life.

Reach for the moon and the stars and be content as often as possible. BREATHE as you go, feel your way to a nicer life and bring forward the real you. We are all waiting and will be so happy to meet you.

The world is full of other people and there are tons of us waiting to meet you.

Conclusion

Oh wow! We have finally made it to the end. Yes, we had to finish our little chat somewhere. There are a few pointers perhaps to remind ourselves from time to time as we have covered a few different areas and time has just flown past. We definitely have looked into some of our own personal stuff.

Our breathing and meditation are of utmost importance to maintain a balance in our emotional and mental well-being. Taking time to breathe can unlock so much about ourselves that it is a vital yet simple practice for us to take part in.

Our meditation and "destressing", again vital though not nearly as vital as it is enjoyable to take our time and set times for ourselves to enjoy allowing our negatives flow out from our self and breathe in the good vibes.

The vibes of our very own minds eye can bring us closer to like-minded people who in turn can help boost us up to reach our goals. When we sense something from others, we need not waste any time in thinking that someone different might show up.

Concentrating on ourselves is a beautiful way in which to allow others into our lives. Those who can benefit us and those who enrich us. The key person to get to know and become a true lover of is SELF. Becoming okay with a journey of self being "selfish" & allowing ourselves to enjoy the person we are & always were.

Let us not forget how important some simple daily exercises can be to our daily life. It is when we hear our own words it can make or break our own build ups to any event or happenings. Not only the words we intend for others. We are also hearing them and so we can always practice by ourselves in private, we can spend our own time in front of our own mirror. Choosing the words we speak to ourselves and by choosing our words we are selecting what we will hear. It is of course important to remember that there are no feelings that will take us completely over and when you have a "thought to yourself" that appears like you have a fear of how you feel. Reach out to a friend. We all in the world love each other in a funny sort of way. I value you in this life of ours. From all of what I have had to walk through is the absolute reason I know you can too.

I am indeed so glad you have taken the time to share with me in my writing journey. You, my readers continue to bring me strength in my journey and provide to me great benefit from your feedback. I am indebted and I do not use my words without choosing carefully.

I hope to hear from you and your thoughts, I am available "normally" on social platforms under my flagship title. @TWOsonsTOOmany (@2sons2manny). Come follow and say "Hi" we can share each other's content more often and be content in having gained a new friend in each other.

I will leave you with one final thought and it is very much a personal piece that I often speak out loud to myself and my son Darra & to my son Patrick. I may have lost them from this life "BUT" I keep them with me every day. My selfishness now is that our relationship now is how I wish to create it. The final thought and something I wish for you to say out loud to yourself daily.

I LOVE YOU!

FOR

Darra, Patrick, Alana

Follow;

Twitter, @TWOsonsTOOmany

Facebook, @TWOsonsTOOmany

Instagram, @2sons2many

Other books by Aidan,

TWO sons TOO many, memoir

17 & Life, memoir

My grief, the last 3 years, poems/blog/short stories.

Printed in Great Britain
by Amazon